Scotch Whisky

Scotch Whisky

as tasted by

Bill Simpson

Anthony Troon

S. Russell Grant

Hugh MacDiarmid

Donald Mackinlay

Jack House

Theodora FitzGibbon

M

SBN 333 17296 5

First published 1974 by Macmillan
Leisure Books, Houndmills, Basingstoke

Made and printed in Great Britain by
Balding + Mansell Ltd, London & Wisbech

CONTENTS

Chapter I

Uisgebaugh

Bill Simpson

If a body could just find oot the exac' proper proportion and quantity that ought to be drunk every day, and keep to that, I verily trow that he might leeve for ever, without dying at a', and that doctors and kirkyairds would go oot o' fashion.

So spoke James Hogg, the Ettrick Shepherd, in all his experienced wisdom when asked to pronounce on his favourite whisky.

But what is this drink that laps the palate of the world? Dr E. C. Barton-Wright wrote in the *New Scientist*:

The production of whisky is undoubtedly an art, and all attempts to produce whisky by a 'scientific' approach have proved to be futile. We have some scientific understanding of the processes involved in making good whisky, yet why Scottish whisky has a characteristic and unique flavour is a complete mystery. Nobody has been able to reproduce it outside Scotland.

The history of distillation is shrouded in the mists of antiquity. According to the Bible, Noah was the first man to discover the potent qualities of wine (Genesis 9.20). The word *alcohol* comes from the Arabic for *pure spirit*. And Aristotle, born in 384 BC, wrote in his *Meteorology*: 'Sea water can be rendered potable by distillation. Wine and other liquids can be subjected to the same process. After they have been converted into humid vapours they return to liquids.'

Despite this welcome expertise, however, legend has it that at the time of the Great Flood one of the ancestors of MacNeil of Barra, whose Kismull stronghold is on a sea-surrounded rock in Castlebay, refused Noah's hospitality, commenting: 'The MacNeil has a boat of his own.'

When and how distilling began in Scotland will never now be known, and the identity of the first maker of Scotch is equally lost in the mirage of time – but the

Order made in 1505 restricting Scotch whisky sales to surgeons and barbers.

Extract from a Scottish Exchequer Roll of 1494, the earliest official reference to Scotch whisky.

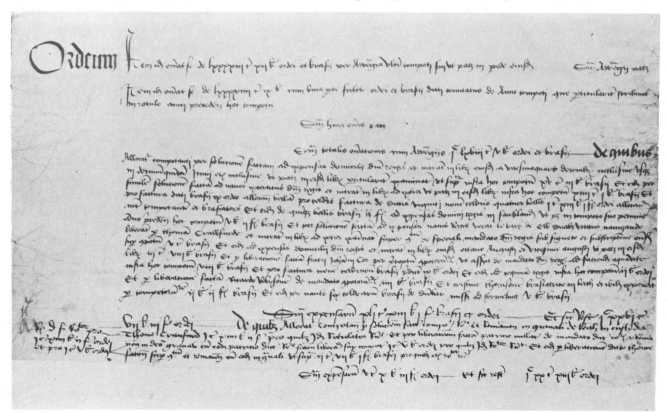

millions of gallons of Scotch maturing in the quiet warehouses of Scotland today are sufficient to float an armada of arks.

Uisgebaugh (pronounced Oohku-bey-a) is Gaelic for 'water of life'. *Uisge* was corrupted first into *Usky* and finally into whisky. Its first recorded mention is in the Scottish Exchequer Rolls for 1494 where there is an entry of 'eight bolls of malt to Friar John Cox wherewith to make *aquavitae*' (Latin for 'water of life').

It is virtually certain, though, that a form of whisky had been produced in Scotland as many as three centuries earlier. The manufacture of spirit was well known in Ireland when that land was first invaded by the English in 1170–2, and it seems highly likely that the art of distillation was brought to Scotland by missionary monks from Ireland. Some of the main centres of distilling, Dufftown and Islay, for instance, were also the sites of early monastic communities.

It was as a medicine that whisky first achieved popularity among the Scots, being prescribed 'for the preservation of health, the prolongation of life, and for the relief of colic, dropsy, palsy and smallpox, as well as a host of other ailments'. It also helped to make a harsh existence bearable.

Other early records are an order from James IV for whisky to be brought to him at Dundee; and in 1505 Edinburgh Town Council tried to restrict the manufacture, sale or use of whisky by decreeing that only surgeons and barbers should be allowed to dispense it.

The first mention of a famous whisky appeared in 1690. This was Ferintosh, already widely noted for its quality when the 'ancient brewery of aquavitie in Cromarty' was destroyed by Jacobites in revenge against Duncan Forbes of Culloden. As compensation, Forbes was allowed to distil free of duty, a privilege that was not finally rescinded until 1784. Meanwhile, Ferintosh flourished. John Knox, writing in 1785, observed that it was 'the sociable practice of Highlandmen in all ages, to seal, ratify, and wash down every compact or bargain, in good old ferintosh'. The whisky's fame was such that it even got an epitaph from Robert Burns, who lamented:

The deil cam fiddlin' throu' the toun,
And danc'd awa wi' th' Exciseman;
                              Burns

Prince Charles Edward Stuart, famous for his leadership of the '45 uprising. His defeat at the battle of Culloden, fought in the same year, opened up the road south and allowed the taste for Scotch to spread gradually to England.

Thee Ferintosh! O sadly lost!
Scotland lament frae coast to coast!
Now colic grips, an' barkin host
      May kill us a',
For loyal Forbes' Charter'd boast
      Is ta'en awa!
Thae curst horse-leeches o' th' Excise,
Wha mak the Whisky stills their prize!
Haud up thy han' Deil! . . . ance, twice, thrice!
      Their seize the blinkers!
An bake them up in brunstane pies
      For poor d' . . . n'd Drinkers.

Scotch spirit was first subjected to government control in 1597 when a famine was feared after a poor barley harvest, and production was temporarily restricted to 'Lords of Barony and Gentlemen of such degree'. And it was not until more than fifty years later, in 1664, that an Act of Excise was passed by the Scots Parliament, fixing the duty at 2s. 8d. per pint for aquavitae or other strong liquor (the Scots pint at the time was approximately one-third of a gallon).

Taxation began a long and turbulent history of smuggling; and as the separate governments of Scotland and England imposed a variety of taxes and other

Two early nineteenth-century illustrations of smuggling.

Overleaf, 'A Highland Whisky Still'; engraving after a painting by Sir Edwin Landseer, 1829.

restrictions over the years, defiance took the form of widespread riots. Revenue Officers were bound and gagged, bribed, even killed; and rioters were 'tried and sentenced to be whipped by the common hangman and transported to the plantations'.

In 1708 – the year after the Union with England – only 50,800 gallons of whisky are known to have been distilled. But by 1758 the amount of duty-paid whisky had increased to 433,800 gallons – and this figure was still a small fraction of the quantities being illicitly distilled. In 1777, for instance, there were 408 stills in Edinburgh – only eight of which were licensed (and there were over two thousand licensed houses to serve a population of 100,000, all but 150 being 'for the lower class of people').

Even in 1820, as a result of short-sighted government administration, there was no legal distillery on Speyside, though a high-class whisky flooded from two hundred illicit stills! Indeed, it was the illicit smugglers who kept, sustained and educated the taste for whisky at a time when legally produced whisky was scarcely worth drinking and licensed distillers were being forced out of business. Their product, sabotaged by taxation, could not compete in quality.

It is significant, too, that the chief centres of illicit whisky production, such as Glenfiddich, became, and still are, the sites for established distillers after the Duke of Gordon, largest landowner in central Scotland at the time, managed to push through the Excise Act of 1823. This enabled licensed distillers, on payment of a reasonable duty, to produce spirit of a strength equal to that made by the smugglers – now the freebooting days were on the wane. The Duke and other landowners promised they would do all they could to suppress illicit distilling – and they did, though the task was immense, and dangerous, with many a 'bloody affray with bands of lawless desperadoes'. Shots were frequently fired, people injured, and killed.

Unfortunately, the Excise Officers were paid grossly inadequate salaries and had to rely on the proceeds of seizure – which they split with the government – for a living. This meant that after a smuggler had been caught, he would be given time to make good his losses before being apprehended again!

Early photographic reconstruction of an illicit whisky still.

Four late nineteenth-century illustrations of illegal distilling.

a A haunt of smugglers.

b The smuggler's cave.

c The export trade.

d The still at work – a quiet cup of tea.

In 1820 Captain Fraser, owner of Brackla Distillery, told the Commissioners of a Parliamentary inquiry that he had 'not sold one hundred gallons for consumption within 120 miles of his residence during the past year, though people drank nothing but whisky.'

Even after the 1823 Act, which incorporated many stiff penalties, had been passed, smuggling continued to flourish – but the Whisky Road and Ladder Trail to Perth and Dundee gradually dried up, though thousands of gallons of illicit whisky were still transported south in pigs' bladders and tin panniers hidden in the voluminous dresses of the smugglers' womenfolk.

The task that faced the Excise can be measured by the fact that more than three thousand detections 'in respect of illicit distilling' were made for the year ending 5 July, 1824, in the Elgin area alone.

Stills were discovered in the most unlikely places – from landlocked caves on the west coast to under the Free Tron Church in Edinburgh's High Street. Even the clock tower still standing in the centre of Dufftown once housed a thriving illicit distillery – though the local Excise Supervisor crossed the square to and from work six days a week!

Gradually, however, the Excise gained the upper hand – and by 1834 smuggling had almost vanished (though a few illicit stills are said to be operating yet).

As battles were won and lost to establish and control production, the amount of spirit drunk was staggering. In 1842 a report by the Committee of the Established Church of Scotland showed that in England fifteen million people consumed almost eight million bottles of spirits (whisky, brandy, gin and rum) – about half a gallon per mouth of the population. Ireland's eight million drank almost 5,300,000 gallons – two-thirds of a gallon each; and in Scotland the population of 2,620,184 celebrated by quaffing more than five and a half million gallons – an average of two gallons per mouth!

Drinking sessions were convened on every conceivable pretext; happiness was 'doled out by the glass and sold by the gill'. Advocates of teetotalism marched the country spreading their message of abstinence, and in 1853 severe restrictions were enforced under the Forbes Mackenzie Act on the opening of licensed premises.

Malt whisky was for centuries the traditional drink of Scotland, but by the very nature of the pot still process, it could only be produced in limited quantities. The development of grain whisky soon after the distillation of Scotch was organised on a commercial scale brought the benefits of large-scale production.

It was in 1826 that Robert Stein of Kilbagie Distillery, Clackmannan, patented an invention which brought the benefits of the Industrial Revolution to the distilling trade. His patent still, superseded in 1830 by an improved version by Aeneas Coffey, an Irish inspector-general of Excise turned distiller, enabled whisky to be made in one continuous operation.

The blending of pot-still malt and patent-still grain whiskies – pioneered about 1860 by Andrew Usher in Edinburgh – gradually altered the industry's structure; and it is this blended product – a product of specialised skill in the selection and marrying of different whiskies – which the world at large recognises in all the famous proprietary brands. Their production, watched over by chemists but more surely judged by experience, is like the breeding of pedigree stock. 'Like must be matched with like, and only time and the most careful selection can ensure a happy creation.'

There is no space here, in this brief historical survey, to tell in detail the fascinating stories of how the famous companies profited from phylloxera – the vine disease that nearly wiped brandy off the drinker's map in the 1880s – and established offices first in London and then around the world. The start of blending was perhaps an even more important cause of the world-wide boom in Scotch.

The marrying of various malt whiskies of different ages and strengths, to grain is much more than a mere formula, though all distillers and blenders have their 'recipe'. It is in this one crucial act that knowledge, experience and instinct combine to produce that sixth-sense which is, perhaps, the real secret of why Scotch has become *the* universal drink, exported to about two hundred countries. In addition, there is the meticulous quality control from the buying of the barley to the choice of site and water – clear, sparkling, the greatest single asset.

Illicit still found in Kintyre, Argyll.

But as exports of Scotch continue to grow, so do attempts to produce a satisfactory imitation. Since 1958 there have been some four hundred cases fought throughout the world by the Scotch Whisky Association, or members of the Association, against bogus brands.

In an attempt, perhaps, to anticipate the permissive age that is sweeping the West, the Japanese attempted to market their version of Scotch with the name King Anne. Even the Soviet Union has had a go. A leaflet issued by Gastronom No. 1, Moscow, states succinctly and sadly: 'The process of preparing sovietsky visky is complex and long.' Let it remain so!

Silver eighteenth-century whisky flask and, below, a silver thistle mug of the same period.

Curiously, it was a Select Committee, set up by the House of Commons in 1890–1, which concluded its investigations of the spirits trade by stating that there was no exact legal definition of spirits going by popular names such as whisky, brandy, rum, potent or silent spirits.

But in November 1905 there occurred one of those seemingly trivial court cases that, in fact, bring about major changes. A Mr Davidge was charged in a North London police court with a contravention of Section 6 of the Food and Drugs Act of 1875.

It was alleged that the pioneering Mr Davidge had sold to the prejudice of the purchaser, who had demanded Scotch whisky, 'something which was not of the nature, substance and quality of Scotch whisky'.

His crime? He had mixed pot-still Scotch malt with Irish whiskey.

The magistrate, Mr W. Snow Fordham, judged that 'the material to be used to produce Scotch whisky is wholly barley malt', and this led to further acrimony and the establishment of the Royal Commission on Whiskey and other Potable Spirits in 1908.

Many 'expert' witnesses were not only prejudiced, but ignorant. The Commission's final report, however, issued on 28 July 1909 sanctified in the 1952 Customs and Excise Act, with further definition in the Finance

Contemporary cartoonist's view of the Royal Commission on Whisky.

Watertight cans used for smuggling whisky to the United States during prohibition.

Act of 1969, basically states: Spirits described as Scotch whisky shall not be deemed to correspond to that description unless they have been obtained by distillation in Scotland from a mash of cereal grain saccharified by the diastase of malt and have been matured in warehouse in cask for a period of at least three years.

Aeneas Macdonald felt that the decision was a 'reckless extension of the term whisky which has had the gravest consequences for the prestige of the industry. It has tended to deprive whisky of the special character it had built up during centuries of careful and pious labour and research.'

But a different view has been expressed recently by James Ross: 'These findings were described as a triumph for the grain distillers, but today, we can look on it only as a victory for common sense.'

The industry had to tighten its belt before, during and after the First World War, especially when Austen Chamberlain raised excise duty to 'give the public the famous 12s. 6d. per bottle'.

Prohibition in America, followed by the depression and the Wall Street collapse of 1929, led to many distillers shutting down; and in the Second World War there were further crises, including the major one of basic supplies. But in 1945 Winston Churchill, with characteristic foresight, minuted for the Ministry of Food:

> On no account reduce the amount of barley for whisky. It takes years to mature and is an invaluable export and dollar earner. Having regard to our difficulties about export, it would be improvident not to reserve this characteristic element of British ascendancy.

After the Second World War there was an acute shortage of stocks of maturing whisky. Because of the importance to the country's economy of foreign currency earnings the Government asked the scotch whisky industry to co-operate in organising a voluntary quota system which would restrict the amount of Scotch put on sale in the home market and then make as much as possible available for export.

The industry agreed and under the quota system sales of Scotch in the United Kingdom were artificially held down right up to 1959. There can be no doubt that as a result Scotch lost some ground in the home market to competing drinks such as gin, which does not need to be matured and can be sold immediately after it has been made. Once stocks had been built up, however, and the quotas removed, Scotch soon regained its position, and today sales of Scotch in Britain are slightly larger in volume than all other spirits, imported as well as domestic, added together.

The 1950s also saw the beginning of a tremendous expansion in the demand for Scotch throughout the world. The United States of America, first to recover from the effects of the war, was the fastest-growing market, and in a very short time sales of Scotch there had far outstripped those at home. Western Europe soon followed this trend and after the removal of import restrictions and the formation of the Common Market, the consumption of Scotch jumped dramatically in France, Western Germany and then Italy. Today Japan appears to be the market with the greatest potential for expansion but the consumption of Scotch continues to expand everywhere.

A number of different explanations have been put forward for this spectacular success story. Some people say it was the American forces who discovered the taste of Scotch during the war and took it back home. Others ascribe the growth in demand to the influence of films, crime stories and even to the spreading vogue for disc-otheques. In all probability there is an element of truth in each of these theories, but in the final instance it is on the unique flavour and character of Scotch, its acceptability as a drink in widely different climates and conditions that its lasting popularity must depend.

Today it is the best-known drink in the world, drunk and appreciated in more than 180 countries. Since the war exports of Scotch have increased by an average of just under 10 per cent a year, and yet larger markets still remain relatively untapped. To meet the growing demand whisky companies have invested vast sums in new distilleries and modern automatic bottling plants. Stocks of maturing whisky in Scotland now stand at the almost incredible figure of over 1,000 million proof gallons, enough to assuage the thirst of the Scots for over three hundred years if they had to drink it all themselves. There seems to be no danger of that, however, which is perhaps just as well not only for the sobriety of the Scots but for the economy of the country.

Display of the best-known whiskies.

Chapter 2

To Live For Ever

Bill Simpson

Whatever the cottage-industry beginnings of Scotland's whisky may have been, Professor David Daiches has shrewdly observed that whisky was a 'life-enhancing spirit' which was 'established in the Scottish imagination well before the seventeenth century'.

In 'The Massacre of the Macpherson', William Aytoun, the nineteenth-century Scottish nationalist and verse-writer, goes further back:

> Fhairson had a son
>   Who married Noah's daughter,
> And nearly spoiled ta Flood
>   By trinking up ta watter,
> Which he would have done –
>   I at least pelieve it,
> Had ta mitxure peen
>   Only half Glenlivet.

Nevertheless, although Scotch has achieved the remarkable success of becoming the most popular international drink, lubricating the small talk of continents, providing solace and occasionally inflaming the wilder passions, it has only rarely excited the professional abilities of poets and writers.

Perhaps the act of swallowing it is sufficient in itself – for whisky and the drinking of it seem to be a compound of opposite extremes, the Caledonian antisyzygy in liquid form.

'Freedom and whisky gang thegither,' was the defiant cry of Robert Burns, whose work has been described as 'essentially bucolic and Bacchanalian in character'.

Apart from 'Tam o' Shanter', where Burns sits with his trusty, drouthy cronies 'bousing at the nappy/An' getting fou and unco happy', he wrote one great drinking song, after surviving a night at Moffat with his old friend Willie Nicol:

> O Willie brew'd a peck o'maut,
>   And Rob and Allan cam to see;
> Three blyther hearts, that lee-lang night,
>   Ye wad na found in Christendie.
>
>   We are na fou, we're nae that fou,
>   But just a drappie in our e'e;
>   The cock may craw, the day may daw,
>   And ay we'll taste the barley bree.
>
> Here are we met, three merry boys,
>   Three merry boys I trow are we;
> And mony a night we've merry been,
>   And mony mae we hope to be!

'Tam o' Shanter' recreated: stone figures of the landlord, Tam himself, Souter Johnie and the landlady in the garden of Souter's cottage.

Robert Burns.

It is the moon, I ken her horn,
    That's blinkin' in the lift sae hie;
She shines sae bright to wyle us hame,
    But by my sooth she'll wait a wee!

Wha first shall rise to gang awa,
    A cuckold coward loun is he!
Wha first beside his chair shall fa',
    He is the king amang us three.

In 'John Barleycorn', a refashioning of an old ballad which tells of the barley's death when it is cut, Burns celebrates with:

John Barleycorn was a hero bold,
    Of noble enterprise,
For if you do but taste his blood,
    'Twill make your courage rise.

The same theme of easily acquired courage is repeated in 'Tam o' Shanter' on that wild winter's night when the auld Kirk of Alloway seemed in a blaze:

Inspiring, bold John Barleycorn!
What dangers thou canst make us scorn!
Wi' tippeny, we fear nae evil;
Wi' usquabae, we'll face the Devil!

And when Westminster laid another of its cursed restrictions on *aquavitae*, by imposing further taxation, Burns parodied Milton to address an 'Earnest Cry and Prayer to the Scotch Representatives in the House of Commons, exorting them to action:

Alas! my roupet Muse is haerse!
Your Honors' hearts wi' grief'twad pierce,
To see her sittin on her arse
                Low i' the dust,
And scriechin out prosaic verse,
                An' like to brust!

In 'Scotch Drink', in which he acknowledges whisky as his Muse, Burns shows his common sense and cynical contempt for the costly time-wasting of lawyers:

When neebors anger at a plea,
An' just as wud as wud can be,
How easy can the barley-bree
                Cement the quarrel!
It's ay the cheapest Lawyer's fee
                To taste the barrel.

Page from a book kept by Burns as an Excise Officer at a distillery. All the entries, except the signature of his superior officer, are in Burns' own hand.

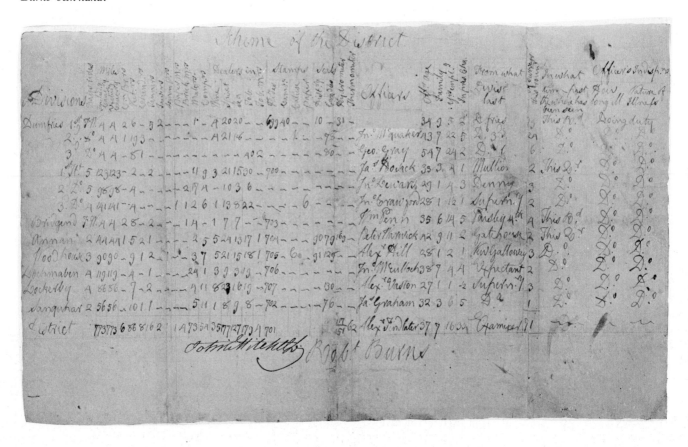

It is doubtful whether there was any recognisable kind of whisky in Solomon's time, but one of Burns' Proverbs showed that the wise man could use it effectively:

Gie him strong Drink until he wink,
   That's sinking in despair;
An' liquor guid to fire his bluid,
   That's prest wi' grief an' care:
There let him bowse, an' deep carouse,
   Wi' bumpers flowing o'er,
Till he forgets his loves or debts,
   An' minds his griefs no more.

Aeneas Macdonald, describing whisky as a 'warlock liquor' which came at the English out of the mists, conjures up a magnificent testimony to this 'potent and princely drink' when he seeks out its mystical and unique appeal:

This swift and fiery spirit . . . belongs to the alchemist's den and to the long nights shot with cold, flickering beams; it is compact of Druid spells and Sabbaths (of the witches and the Calvinists); its graces are not shameless, Latin, and abundant, but have a sovereign austerity, whether the desert's or the north wind's; there are flavours in it, insinuating and remote, from mountain torrents and the scanty soil on moorland rocks and slanting, rare sun-shafts.

As an enthusiastic connoisseur, Macdonald was constantly elaborating, caressing and whipping the language in an attempt to keep pace with the 'purest and noblest' of national drinks:

Whisky – even inferior whisky – has a potency and a directness in the encounter which proclaims its sublime rank. It does not linger to toy with the senses, it does not

One of the most popular Edinburgh taverns, Johnny Dowie's in Libberton's Wynd, frequented by Robert Burns.

Overleaf: late eighteenth-century drinking scene.

seep through the body to the brain; it communicates through no intermediary with the core of a man, with the roots of his consciousness; it speaks from deep to deep. This quality of spiritual insistency derives from the physical nature of the liquid. Whisky is a re-incarnation; it is made by a sublimation of coarse and heavy barley malt; the spirit leaves that earthly body, disappears, and by a lovely metapsychosis returns in the form of a liquid exquisitely pure and impersonal. And thence whisky acquires that lightness and power which is so dangerous to the unwary, and so delightful to those who use it with reverence and propriety.

This feeling of reverence and release from materialism is also noted by R. H. Bruce Lockhart:

Throughout the ages whisky has been an integral part of the Celtic civilization. . . . It was a noble spirit, a symbol of independence, to be approached with reverence, and, in spite of the changes wrought by blending, the Celts have communicated something of this reverence to the whole Scottish nation.

Novelist Neil Gunn, an Exciseman like Burns before him, was also lyrical, feeling that single malt whiskies, with their individual flavours,

recall the world of hills and glens, of raging elements, of shelter, of divine ease. The perfect moment of their reception is after bodily stress – or mental stress, if the body be sound. The essential oils that wind in the glass then uncurl their long fingers in lingering benediction and the whole works of creation are made manifest. At such a moment the basest man would bless his enemy.

He is equally impressive in the flowing sincerity of his eloquence when he describes the making of whisky:

Round the southern corner of the dun there was a field of barley all ripened by the sun. In a small wind it echoed faintly the sound of the ocean; at night it sighed and rustled as the earth-mother thought things over, not without a little anxiety. It was cut and harvested and a sheaf offered in thanksgiving; flailed and winnowed; until the ears of grain remained in a heap of gold: the bread of life.

In simple ways the grain was prepared and ground and set to ferment; the fermented liquor was then noiled, and as the steam came off it was by happy chance condensed against some cold surface.

And lo! this condensation of steam from the yellowish-green fermented gruel is clear as crystal. It is purer than any water from any well. When cold, it is colder to the fingers than ice.

A marvellous transformation! A perfect water. But in the mouth – what is this? The gums tingle, the throat burns, down into the belly fire passes, and thence outward to the finger-tips, to the feet, and finally to the head . . . . Clearly it was not water he had drunk: it was life.

Dr Johnson, who first tasted whisky in 1773, during his tour of the Hebrides with James Boswell. On the island of Coll, Boswell relates, 'whisky was served round in a shell, according to the ancient Highland custom'.

Another Exciseman and author, Maurice Walsh, writing in 1950, proclaimed:

> After all, my acquaintanceship with Scotch has lasted only a matter of a mere forty-nine years, and you need half-a-century at least to claim some knowledge.

A whiff of Standfast, however, was enough to allow him to see a vision:

> I see the long-winding valley with the chimney stalks and kiln-pagodas above the trees; I see the Fiddich and the Dullan running fast and clear over bright gravel, the bald Convals fringed with a hair of pines, big Ben Rinnes with cap atilt over the glen; I smell again the peat, the wash, and the feints, and feel the tightness of carbon-dioxide in my throat; and I see myself getting out of a warm bed in the dark of a Januar' morning. And I see a girl with red hair.

There is a darker, poorer side to Scotland, a hard urban life far removed from lyrical visions. Condemning the slums of Glasgow as the most powerful ally of death and disease, George Malcolm Thomson thundered:

> From scenes like these auld Scotia's grandeur, in its present battered condition, springs! From the shadowed courts and perpetually darkened rooms of this empire on which the sun never rises, from these evil-smelling, death-haunted tenements in which half a people lives, from the filth, despair, and promiscuity of the slums the latest generation of Scots is emerging. The wonder is not that Scotland has more crime than England but that there is an honest man or decent woman to be found among this sunken half-nation; not that there is drunkenness but that there is sobriety. 'The Drink Trade!' For years the pious, patronizing middle classes have been pointing to it as the enemy, the malign force that called the slums into being. But there may be conditions of life so monstrous that drink is the only refuge from the intolerable burden of conscious misery, the only defiance left to outraged human dignity.

Slum-dwellers were not alone in their need, or delight, in drink. In the cellars of various taverns

> lords, lawyers, lairds met and had their high jinks, and the mirth was loud and the stories and jests were broad. In one room might be assembled judges relaxing their intellects after deciding subtle points on feudal law, while in the other their clerks caroused, retailing their lordships' Parliament House jokes of yesterday. Lords of Session might indulge with impunity in bacchanalian nights, and waken with brain clear to unravel an intricate case of multiplepoinding next morning; but such ongoings played sad havoc with feebler constitutions. They ruined the health of poor Robert Fergusson the poet, and were more than even Robert Burns could stand in too frequent and too late sittings at the Crochallan Club or in the tavern of John Dowie – most sauve of hosts – where judges resorted for their 'meridian' in the day, and impecunious men of letters assembled at night, sitting in the narrow little room ominously named the 'coffin'.

Robert Fergusson.

Indeed, it is said that Burns exclaimed on his deathbed

> O these Edinburgh gentles–it if hadna been for them I had a constitution would have stood onything!'

And before he died in 1774 on the straw of a madhouse, at the age of twenty-four, Fergusson's poetical innovations had shown genius. Burns' debt to him is enormous. In the 'King's Birth-Day in Edinburgh' Fergusson writes:

> O Muse, be kind, and dinna fash us,
> To flee awa' beyont Parnassus,
> Nor seek for Helicon to wash us,
>   That heath'nish spring;
> Wi' Highland whisky scour our hawses
>   And gar us sing.

It was Marian McNeill in *The Scots Cellar* who was happy to point out that although hospitality and conviviality are not the same thing,

> in Scotland they are inextricably mingled. The Scots have always been a highly convivial folk, and every social occasion used to centre round a tappit-hen, brimming with claret, a reeking punch-bowl, a grey-beard of malt whisky, or a bowie reaming with home-brewn ale.

After-dinner conversation.

The tradition of hospitality continues still, and the liberality of a man's disposition is often judged by his manner in dispensing whisky.

Two Highlanders were discussing a gentleman of their acquaintance. 'What ails ye at him, Duncan?' asked one of them.

'Och, I wass up at his house last week, and he wass pouring me out a glass of whisky, and of course I said, "Stop!" – and man, wad ye belive it, he stoppit!'

Indeed, as Marian McNeill has gone on to point out, 'in rural communities copious libations of the national beverages – ale and whisky – attended each and all from the cradle to the grave'.

Sometimes, indeed, beyond the grave, for funerals have often been more hectic and amusing than weddings – a unique blend of mourning and merry-making which occasionally found the mourners in a state of funereal hilarity or sodden solemnity at the grave with the corpse left behind.

Funerals are more sober affairs nowadays, though a Scottish wake can still be awe-inspiring to the un-initiated or to those used to drinking mere glass-dampening measures of one-sixth. Dean Ramsay, Dean of Edinburgh from 1846 and author of *Reminiscences of Scottish Life and Character*, a popular collection of Scottish stories and anecdotes, recalls that

There was a sort of infatuation in the supposed dignity and manliness attached to powers of deep potation, and the fatal effects of drinking were spoken of in a manner both reckless and unfeeling.

Thus, I have been assured that a well-known old laird of the old school expressed himself with great indignation at the charge brought against hard drinking that it had actually *killed* people. 'Na, na, I never knew onybody killed wi' drinking, but I hae ken'd some that deed in the training.

Dr John Strang, in *Glasgow and its clubs*, tells of

Scottish galraviches, as these drinking-bouts were called. Well known to all acquainted with the 'annals of the bottle', and the one in which Garscadden took his last draught has been often told. The scene occurred in the wee clachan of Law, where a considerable number of Kilpatrick lairds had congregated for the ostensible purpose of talking over some parish business. And well they talked and better they drank, when one of them, about the dawn of the morning, fixing his eye on Garscadden, remarked that he was looking 'unco gash' (ghastly). Upon which Kilmardinny coolly replied, 'Deil mean him, since he has been wi' his Maker these twa hours. I saw him step awa, but I didna like to disturb good company!

Although ministers and elders have little to learn about drinking, they were always constantly inveighing against its 'evil effects' – as they still do today. This protest by the Presbytery of Penpont in 1736 is typical:

Yet further how unaccountable and scandalous are the large gatherings and unbecoming behaviour at burials and lake-wacks, also in some places how many are grossly un-mannerly in coming to burials without invitations. How extravagant are many in their preparations for such occa-sions, and in giving much drink, and driving it too frequent-ly before and after the corpse is enterred, and keeping the company too long together; how many scandalouslie drink untill they be drunk on such occasions; this practice can-not but be hurtfull, therefore ought to be discouraged and reformed, and people that are not ashamed to be so vilely unmannerly as to thrust themselves into such meetings without being called ought to be affronted.

One of the most famous funeral scenes in all literature appears in Tobias Smollett's *Humphry Clinker*.

Yesterday we were invited to the funeral of an old lady . . . , and found ourselves in the midst of fifty people, who were regaled with a sumptuous feast, accompanied with the music of a dozen pipers. In short, this meeting had all the air of a grand festival; and the guests did such honour to the entertainment, that many of them could not stand when they were reminded of the business on which we had met. . . .

The body was committed to the earth, the pipers playing a pibroch all the time, and all the company standing un-covered. The ceremony was closed with the discharge of pistols; then we returned to castle, resumed the bottle, and by midnight there was not a sober person in the family, the females excepted . . . . Our entertainer was a little chagrined at our retreat, and afterwards seemed to think it a dis-paragement to his family, that not above an hundred gallons of whisky had been drank upon such a solemn occasion.

The 'wee German lairdie', King George IV, may have appeared ridiculous in his kilt when he arrived in

Edinburgh in 1822, but his good taste and education lacked nothing so far as whisky was concerned.

In *Memoirs of a Highland Lady*, Elizabeth Grant of Rothiemurchus tells of an incident that angered her at the time:

> Lord Conyngham, the Chamberlain, was looking everywhere for pure Glenlivet whisky: the King drank nothing else. It was not to be had out of the Highlands. My father sent word to me – I was the cellarer – to empty my pet bin, where was whisky long in wood, long in uncorked bottles, mild as milk, and the true contraband *gout* in it. Much as I grudged this treasure it made our fortunes afterwards, showing on what trifles great events depend. The whisky, and fifty brace of ptarmigan all shot by one man, went up to Holyrood House, and were graciously received and made much of, and a reminder of this attention at a proper moment by the gentlemanly Chamberlain ensured to my father the Indian Judgeship.

It is ironical that Scotland, still suffering from a Calvinist hangover, has to put up with some of the most stupid licensing laws ever enacted – they well exemplify the Holy Willie hypocrisy of so many Scottish Members of Parliament.

'Whisky, no doubt, is a devil, but why has this devil so many worshippers?' asked Lord Cockburn. It is not a question the clergy are likely to answer.

The tax on whisky, which is still grossly unfair, has aroused the anger of many, as Eric Linklater has testified:

> The tax on whisky is manifestly a stupid tax. It appears also to be a malevolent tax. One cannot believe it would continue at its present monstrous figure if distilling were an English industry – or should one call it an art?

And Neil Gunn was equally bitter:

> The discrimination against whisky is so manifestly unjust that it does have the appearance of being deliberately vindictive....

Drinking the health of the Duke of Rothesay with Highland honours at the dinner of the Highland Society, 1872.

Whisky may encourage, indeed induce, a state of lewdness – but there is little evidence to this effect observed and noted down, though an old saying simply states a fundamental truth: 'There are two things that a Highlander likes naked, and one is malt whisky.'

A Gaelic toast in praise of whisky is more explicit:

> Is coisiche na h-oidhche thu
> Gu leapannan na maighdeannan;
> A Righ! gur h-iomadh loinn a th'ort
> Gu coibhneas thoirt a gruagach.

> You are the prowler of the night
> To the beds of virgins;
> O God! what powers you have
> To gain kindness from girls.

And its effects may be equally startling. A wit, long anonymous, observed:

> We're a' dry wi' the drinkin' o't,
> We're a' dry wi' the drinkin' o't,
> The minister kisst the fiddler's wife,
> He couldna preach for thinkin' o't.

During the great festival of Hogmanay, many people remember nothing further than awakening in the morning 'on an alien lobby mat', for as Will Ogilvie put it:

> When the last big bottle's empty and the dawn
>   creeps grey and cold,
> And the last clan-tartan's folded and the last
>   damned lie is told;
> When they totter down the footpaths in a braw
>   unbroken line,
> To the peril of the passers and the tune of
>   'Auld Lang Syne',
> You can tell the folk at breakfast as you watch the
>   fearsome sicht,
> They've only been assisting at a braw Scots Nicht!

Equally typical, as Marion McNeil recalls, is the predicament of the Glasgow undergraduate who, trying to make his way home in the wee sma' oors of Ne'er Day, encountered a lamp-post, made several futile attempts to get past it, and was heard to mutter: 'Losht, losht! Losht in an impenetrable foresht!'

And a last word from poet and author Alexander Scott, who has recently written a series of epigrams – *Scotched* – which puncture the fantasy balloons of myth and fact grown grotesque by the 'wha's like us?' syndrome.

Scotch Optimism	*Scotch Pessimism*	*Scotch Drink*
Through a gless,	Nae	Nip
Darkly.	Gless.	Trip.

Hogmanay in Edinburgh.

Harry Lauder, the Glasgow music-hall artiste. His tribute to whisky 'Just a wee deoch and doris' must be one of the first versions of 'one for the road'.

30

A cartoonist's view of the distillery: two Heath Robinson drawings, specially commissioned by Johnnie Walker.

Chapter 3

Land of Scotch

Anthony Troon

Of all Scotland's mysteries, by far the greatest and most pleasurable is the strange and inexplicable sorcery which is set to work in the distilling of Scotch whisky.

The elements in this sorcery spring from the country itself – its water, its air, its living plants, the nature of its earth and rock. Each of these gives to Scotch whisky something of itself in indefinable, immeasurable qualities, to add to the traditional skill of distilling which has mysteries and imponderable elements of its own.

But unlike the whisky itself, the sorcery does not travel. The most careful, scientifically controlled attempts to duplicate Scotch whisky outside Scotland have produced only dismal and instantly recognisable counterfeits.

It takes the fire and water and air of Scotland to make Scotch. The barley itself – a very hardy cereal well suited to the Scottish climate – is nowadays often augmented by grain brought from outside. But it is the fire and the water that give to each malt whisky most of its individual personality.

Drawing its character from Scotland, whisky gives much in return, sustaining communities where no other work is available. Today whisky is the fifth largest employer of labour in manufacturing in Scotland and many thousands more are indirectly dependent on the world's thirst – in agriculture, bottle-making, packaging, transport, every skill necessary to conduct a highly competitive, and successful, international business.

Geographically, Scotland can be divided roughly into the Highlands, the Lowlands and the Islands. In each of these areas, deposits of peat have been laid down in varying amounts as the rich forests of past ages become the moorlands of today. It is logical that this traditional and readily available fuel from the country's hearth should provide the element of fire in whisky distilling. The faint taste and aroma of its 'reek' is the gift that peat gives to many malt whiskies.

In all its contrasting regions, Scotland is a land of water. Its many rivers are fed by countless burns, and this water – uncontaminated by the chemical additives which intervene between the river and the household tap – is taken straight into the distillery. To the distiller, his traditional source of free-running water is a priceless asset. Those who are knowledgeable about Scottish malts say that the water is the strongest factor in giving each whisky its individuality of flavour and bouquet. It is the water which, on its path from the hills, collects subtle elements of the Scottish environment so that an unmistakable stamp of the land itself is distilled into the national drink.

It is not too fanciful to believe that whiskies embody the character of the different regions. Lowland whiskies are mild and equable, like the gentle countryside in which they are made. Islay whiskies have the tang of the sea spray that washes the island. From the desolate highlands come whiskies with a flavour redolent of honey and of the rich peat in which over thousands of years the essence of heather, gorse and pure trees have been compressed.

Many of the largest group – the Highland malts – are born in the region of Strathspey, the region in which Scotland's second longest river winds from the heights of Badenoch to the lush coastal plain east of Inverness. Early in its course, the Spey's horizons are enclosed by the Cairngorm and Monadhliath mountain ranges; later, it and its tributaries meet the cluster of Speyside distilleries and get down to the business of whisky.

Nowhere else is whisky taken so seriously as in Dufftown, which is recognised as the 'capital' of malt distilling. An old rhyme recalls the time when it had as many stills as Rome had hills; but it remains a small town, set in a bowl in the hills and equipped with enough clan history to furnish it with two nearby castles. One of these, Balvenie Castle, was among the earliest stone castles in the country. Another whisky town of Strathspey, Aberlour, lives just as quietly in the palm of the hills, overlooked by two major peaks, Ben Rinnes and Ben Aigan.

One of the charms of Highland malt distilling is that it remains a rural industry, the distinctive pagoda towers which indicate its presence set down on moorlands, in glens and in small towns. An exception is a distillery at Wick, in the far north, better known perhaps

The pure water of Scotland, one of the essential elements of Scotch Whisky.

Balvenie Castle.

The magnificent Spey, seen from Fochabers Bridge, Morayshire.

for fishing and glass-making. The town's name, derived from the Norse, tells of its importance as an early settlement; its two harbours speak of the great silver-rush of the last century when the Scots became fishermen in a big way, following the herring shoals around their rocky coasts.

From the central group on Speyside, the Highland malt distilleries stretch up and down Scotland's east coast, where hills rise smoothly from the North Sea's edge to the wilder regions inland. But in the desolate and more remote west there are distilleries too, at Fort William and Oban. The first of these towns stands below the rounded brow of Britain's highest mountain, Ben Nevis, at the western mouth of the Caledonian Canal. This mighty chain of loch and waterway, cutting through the country to Inverness in the east, is having a second honeymoon now as a centre for pleasure craft. Fort William itself is a comparatively new town, developed during the last century on what had already been a strategic military site for two hundred years.

The fishing port and steamer centre of Oban mixes its whisky with an entirely different environment. Here, holiday hotels form a well-behaved crescent beside a busy harbour. Behind, Battery Hill is crowned with a curious structure, a skeletal birthday cake called MacCaig's folly, an abortive piece of philanthropy from the 1890s.

These are the many and varied environments of the Highland malts. The Lowland malt whiskies, in their own way, spring from equally diverse surroundings. Fewer in number, the distilleries are grouped around Scotland's industrial centre, with one 'rogue' distillery far to the south in Wigtownshire. The valley of the Forth and Clyde has seen much of Scotland's history. Here – at Stirling, Linlithgow and Edinburgh – were the seats of its monarchs. Today the signs of the past merge with those of modern industrial effort. One distillery, at Bowling in Dunbartonshire, stands where the present-day embroilment of the oil industry meets the Roman remains of Antoninus' Wall. Falkirk, an important centre in the industrial belt, was the site of two great battles in the thirteenth and eighteenth centuries; today, its attentions are concentrated on the heavy work of the twentieth.

The Lowlands these may be by name: but almost every square yard of Scotland enjoys a view of hills or mountains, and there are plenty of hilly spines here – the Cheviots, the Lammermuirs and the Lowther Hills, which carry on their backs some of the highest villages in the country.

The Campbeltown whiskies, now the smallest of the four malt families, come from surroundings where the sea tends to occupy a large part of the horizon,

Unloading the catch at Port Ellen, Islay.

Campbeltown harbour.

Overleaf: Cutting peat, the Falls of Braan at Dunkeld, Perthshire, and the Sound of Mull, Argyllshire.

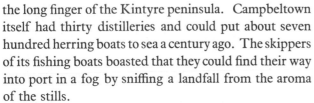
Stacking peat before transport to the maltings.

The River Tay at Perth Bridge.

the long finger of the Kintyre peninsula. Campbeltown itself had thirty distilleries and could put about seven hundred herring boats to sea a century ago. The skippers of its fishing boats boasted that they could find their way into port in a fog by sniffing a landfall from the aroma of the stills.

The most southerly of the Hebrides, Islay, has secured for itself a special place in the story of whisky. There are no fewer than eight distilleries taking their water from this peaty and salt-tasting island, only twenty-five miles along its greatest length.

There may be some connection between distilling and song, for, like Skye, Islay is a traditional home of singers and bards. Once it was the administrative centre of the Lordship of the Isles, and ancient stone crosses recall times beyond the rule of the Vikings. Sliced almost through by the sea-loch Indaal, Islay rises to its highest point at Scaribh Hill, 1,197 feet high, running down to green pastures, brown and gold moorlands and enchanting white beaches fringed with machair.

But for the main centres of grain whisky and blending, you must look again to the mainland. Two lie along the River Tay; Perth and Dundee are places of completely contrasting character for all their neighbourliness. Perth is symptomatic of the blender's art, for here the highlands meet and merge with the Lowlands. Unlike many Scots county towns, Perth seems to have retained a sense of quiet bustle, its flat panorama punctuated by spires and open places. Its bridges gracefully loop the Tay, overlooking islands where Bonnie Prince Charlie

worked up his soldiers for two failed but unforgotten rebellions.

Where the Tay meets the sea, Dundee puts on a workaday face of factories and docks. This is one of Scotland's four cities, and one of very independent mind. Its traditional industries have saddled it with a disposition for jute, jam and journalism, but Dundee can also turn its hand to postcards, offshore oil and some fine blended whiskies.

Of the other two major centres, Glasgow commands one-fifth of Scotland's population, one million people, in an ever-changing and ever-developing industrial complex. So much has Glasgow changed down the centuries that only one house, built in the fifteenth century, still stands to recall its prominence as an ecclesiastical and trading centre of the Middle Ages. But some delightful Victorian buildings in the city centre demonstrate the first period of its big expansion. All around, the battlefield of motorways and high flats under construction show its willingness to reshape itself for the future.

Edinburgh, a city beloved by tourists, is the home of Scottish banking and law, and clings to its title of 'Athens of the North' despite attempts to deface it. With its Royal park in the centre, overlooked by the dead volcano called Arthur's Seat, and its rock-poised castle and palace joined by the backbone of the Royal Mile, Edinburgh has perhaps too many visual benefits to be true. And here again, the business of whisky is part of tradition and part of the present.

The industrial lowlands, with their large population and good transport facilities, are the centre of the blending and bottling industries. Above, Glasgow old and new: left, a new high-rise housing development and, right, the view across the river Clyde to Carlton Place. Below, Edinburgh Castle and the National Gallery of Scotland.

The Glenfiddich and Balvenie distilleries at Dufftown. Though these distilleries use the same water, barley and manufacturing techniques, the two malts produced are recognisably different – proof enough of the strange chemistry of Scotch whisky.

Laphroaig distillery, Islay.

The still house at Auchentoshan distillery.

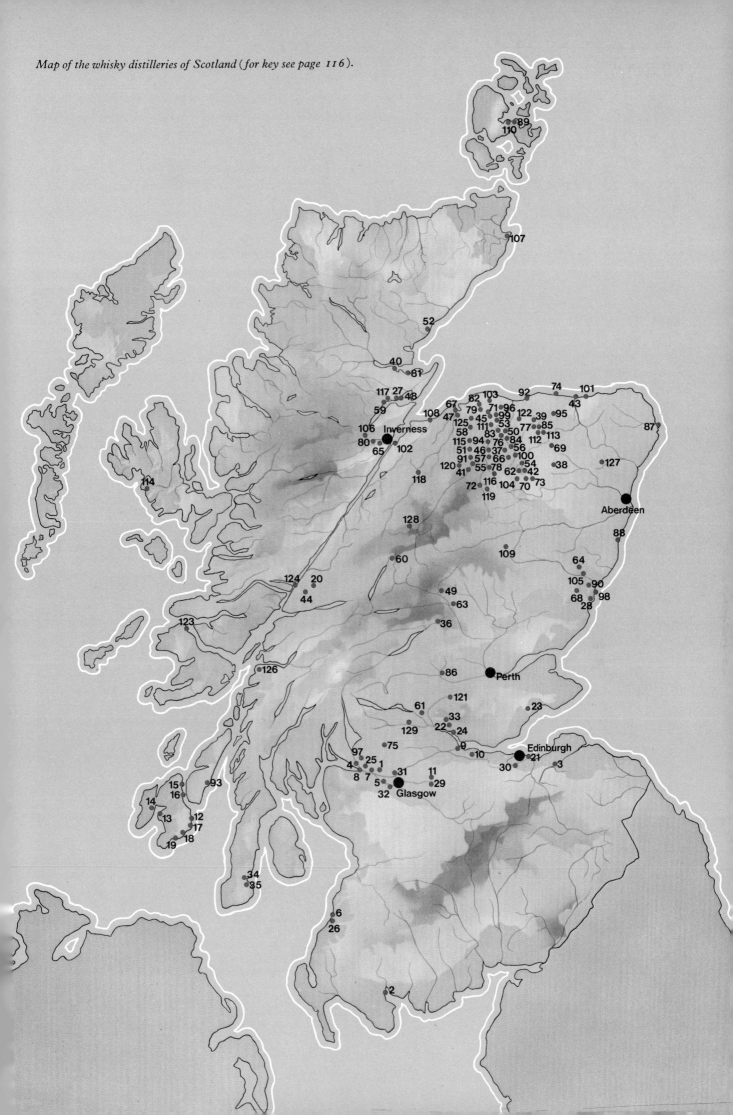

Map of the whisky distilleries of Scotland (for key see page 116).

Chapter 4

Mystery or Myth

S. Russell Grant

production director, Glenlivet Distillers Ltd

Making whisky is a tranquil and leisurely craft. Distilleries are peaceful places, where the few people to be seen go about their work almost casually, as though confident that they can well leave the stills to get on with the business of distillation. And the stills themselves are surprisingly uncomplicated pieces of machinery, designed one might think more for aesthetic pleasure than for functional efficiency. Yet distillation, although practised by man for thousands of years, remains one of the most obscure industrial processes, with many facets that even now are not wholly understood or explained.

Set half-a-dozen samples of Scotch whisky in front of a group of distillers and they will argue long into the night, not so much about the merits of the whisky but about whether by some change in the choice of grain, the timing of the process or the length or method of maturation, a different result might have been achieved.

Some may suspect that this is not so much mystery as mystique, perpetuated by distillers for commercial reasons to preserve the prestige of their product. In actual fact a great amount of research has been carried out by whisky companies, designed not only to find improved and more efficient methods of distilling but to learn more about the nature of the spirits they produce. The latest techniques of analysis have discovered some three hundred different constituents in whisky, and scientists believe that there may be another hundred or so which have not yet been identified.

The techniques used by the distillers in this Renaissance engraving are much the same in principle as those practised today, and indeed basic methods have changed little over many hundreds of years.

Ioan. Stradanus invent.   Phls Galle excud.

A The Still	L A Pewter Crane
B The Worm tub	M A Pewter Valencia
C The Pump	N Hippocrates bag or Flannel
D Water tub	Sleeve
E A Press	O Poker Fire-shovel Cole rake
FFF Tubs to hold the goods	P A Box of Bungs
GGGG Canns of different size	Q The Worm within the Worm tub
H A Wood Funnel with a iron nosel	mark'd with prick'd lines
I A large Vessel to put the Fains	R A Piece of Wood to keep down
or after runnings	the Head of the Still to
K Tin pump	prevent flying of

Engraving showing a whisky distillery in 1729.

Ripened barley ready for the harvest. Today, distillers buy much of their barley outside Scotland, for geographical origin is less important than a barley with the correct properties.

Stirring the barley in a steep to promote germination.

Turning the barley on the malting floor to control its temperature and secure an even rate of germination.

'Ploughing' the barley on the malting floor.

Sprouting barley after it has been turned. Its growth will now be halted by drying it in the kiln.

Stoking the kiln with peat. Here, as the barley is dried, it absorbs the unique flavour and fragrance of the peat.

The pagoda chimney, a landmark throughout Scotland, acts as an open ventilator, drawing hot air from the furnace through the green malt on the kiln floor.

Once kilned, the malt must be ground in a mechanical mill. Here a maltster checks that the consistency and composition of the 'grist' is suitable for mashing.

It is the combination of these constituents in varying proportions that produces the wide range of different flavours to be found in Scotch whisky. Since the number of combinations is virtually infinite and since, in any case, taste is purely subjective and incapable of measurement, it is impossible to know with precise certainty what gives a whisky its character or to lay down standards and rules for distillation.

A distiller knows from the accumulated experience of generations or even centuries how he can produce a whisky with certain characteristics. This is the whisky for which his distillery is known, and when he places his order the blender must be able to rely on obtaining a whisky with exactly those characteristics. Consistency is therefore all important, and this is the reason why the distilling of Scotch whisky has remained a traditional process with few major changes over several hundred years. In the past those who experimented often discovered, to their cost, that new methods altered the character of their whisky without necessarily improving it. As a result distillers have always been reluctant to make any changes in their processes or equipment, some even carrying this reluctance so far as to forbid walls to be painted or cobwebs swept away in case the whisky might be affected.

Improvements have, of course, taken place in distilleries for greater efficiency or economy, but these have mainly been in ancillary processes such as malting, in the use of instruments as an aid to control or in the handling of casks. The only significant change in distilling itself over the past hundred years has been in the method by which the stills are heated. Otherwise whisky today is made by the same processes and in the same kind of equipment that the farmer or the illicit distiller were using several hundred years ago.

Two kinds of whisky are made in Scotland today. Malt whisky is produced in the traditional pot still, and grain whisky is made in the patent still, invented and developed in the 1830s. In both processes the principle of distillation is the same, as of course it is for the production of all spirits, but the equipment used and the scale of operations in each case differ considerably.

By law **malt whisky** can be produced only from malted barley, and the complete process required to make it can conveniently be divided into five stages: malting, mashing, fermentation, distillation and maturation.

The distiller has to exercise his skill and judgment before even the first of these operations can be started,

Delivering barley to a distillery, c. 1870.

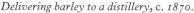

when he is buying his barley.. Only two or three species of barley are suited to making whisky, and the age, colour, formation and moisture content of the grain must be taken into account when deciding whether it will give the required yield and will be easily manageable.

Malt can be made in several ways. Floor maltings, once a traditional part of every distillery, are becoming rarer since they cannot meet the requirements of large-scale production. In them, however, the process is easy to watch and understand, and they thus provide the best illustration of the principle of malting, which is the same no matter what method is used. The barley is first 'steeped' or soaked in water for between two and three days, following which it is spread over the floor of the maltings. Here it begins to germinate and as it does so certain chemical changes take place in the grain, the essence of which is that the starch is modified into a form of sugar to feed the young plant.

The rate of germination is carefully controlled by turning the barley at regular intervals by hand, using wooden shovels known as 'shiels'. The rhythmic skill of the men who turn the malt makes this a most picturesque operation, fascinating to watch, and many will regret its gradual disappearance. Most of the malt used

by the whisky industry today is produced either in saladin boxes or in drum maltings, where the germinating barley is turned mechanically.

In any case, whatever the process used, germination must be stopped once it has developed far enough. This is done by drying the barley, or 'green malt', as it is now called, in a kiln. The floor of the kiln on which the green malt is spread is perforated, allowing the hot air and smoke from a furnace underneath to percolate upwards through the grain. Peat is the traditional fuel for this furnace, and the peat smoke imparts to the malt its characteristic flavour, which can later be discerned in the whisky. Once the malt has absorbed as much of the 'peat reek' as the distiller thinks fit, peat is replaced by coke in the furnace to complete the drying of the grain as quickly and efficiently as possible.

Peat has an important influence on the flavour and character of the whisky produced by a distillery. There is considerable variation in peats that are cut in different parts of Scotland, and those from the islands or coastal areas of the mainland, for example, give a smoke with a much more pungent aroma that can be readily identified in the whiskies. Conservationists as well as anxious whisky lovers sometimes express concern at the considerable quantities of peat currently being used by the

Floor maltings are gradually disappearing and in many cases the barley is now turned mechanically, either in Saladin maltings, shown here, or in drum maltings.

Testing the temperature inside a malt kiln.

47

Filling an open mash tun with hot water and grist.

Opposite, testing the 'wash' – the crude alcohol that results from fermentation – at the wash-back.

In the mash tun mechanical stirrers mash the grist and hot water to produce a sugary liquid suitable for fermentation.

Fermentation takes place in large vats known as wash-backs. Here the liquid from the mash tun (worts) is seen running into a wash-back where yeast is added and fermentation begins.

Two early prints showing malt being ground and a mash tun illustrate how little methods and equipment have altered over the centuries.

industry. There is, however, more peat in Scotland than meets the eye, and experts estimate that even if whisky distilling continues to increase at its present rate of growth, the country's reserves will last for at least another thousand years.

Because of the rapid growth in the demand for Scotch whisky throughout the world, most malt whisky distilleries have greatly extended their distilling capacity, and few of them would be able to make enough malt for their needs at the distillery by floor malting alone. Today more and more malt is being produced in centralised maltings which are highly automated and have an output large enough to cater for several distilleries. Other distillers buy their malt from professional maltsters outside the industry. In either case the malt is made to specifications given by the distiller which lay down, among other things, how heavily it should be 'peated'.

The next step towards making whisky is to convert the dried malt into a sugary liquid which can be fermented. Before this can be done, the malt must first be ground in a mill. Ground malt, which is known in the trade as 'grist', resembles a very coarse flour with the husk of grain mixed up in it. Milling is also an operation calling for skill and experience, for the proportions of

flour and husk in the grist must be carefully regulated to obtain the maximum yield while at the same time the mixture must be prevented from becoming too difficult to handle.

Extraction takes place in the mash tun, a large circular vessel made of metal with a false, perforated bottom. In it the grist is mixed with hot water and stirred by a revolving stirrer. The liquid is drained off and the process repeated with two further waters to make sure that all the soluble spirit is extracted from the grist. The last of these waters is very weak in strength and is held back to be used as the first water of the next mash. The fermenting room contains a number of large cylindrical vessels known as wash-backs, these are usually made of larch, although stainless steel is sometimes now used. Liquid from the mash tun or 'worts' is run into these vessels, a measured quantity of yeast is added and fermentation begins. The enzymes in the yeast begin to attack the sugar in the worts and the reaction is so violent that the liquid starts to bubble, forming a growth that would rise over the top of the wash-backs were it not for the action of revolving switchers which keep cutting off the 'head' as long as fermentation continues. After about thirty-six to forty hours the worts have been turned into a crude form of

When the yeast attacks the sugar in the worts a violent reaction results, causing the liquid to bubble vigorously.

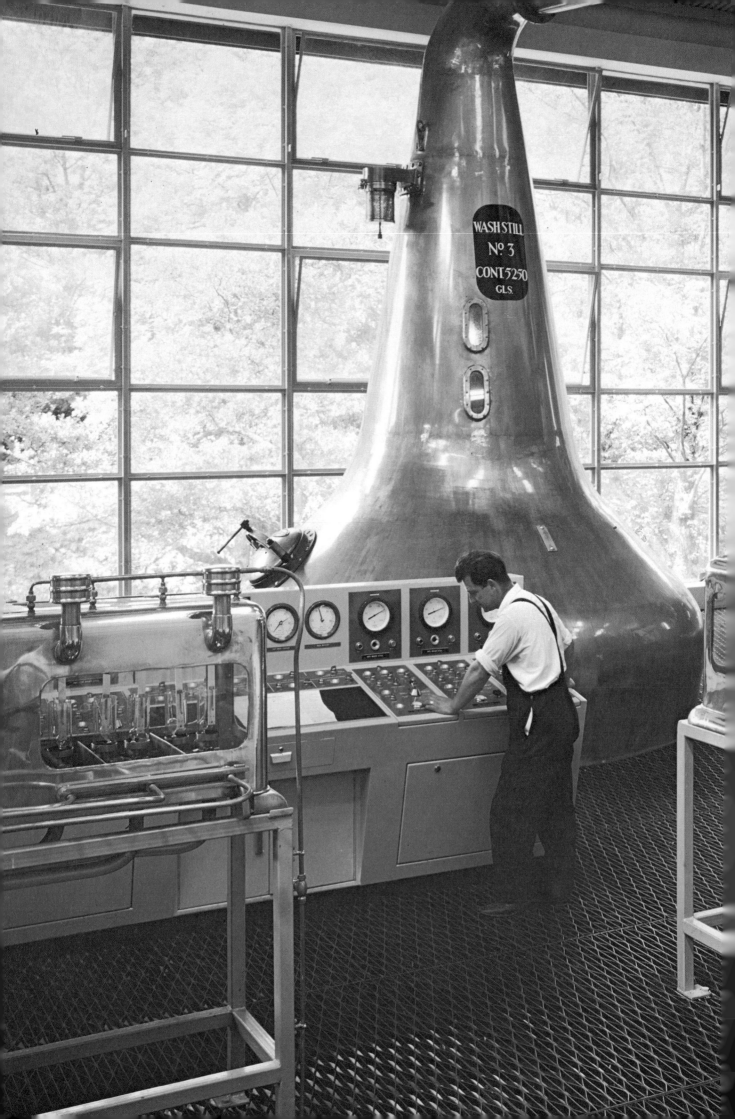

An excise officer locks a still: once alcohol is produced it must remain in bond until, many years later, it is bottled for dispatch to the customer.

Testing the alcoholic strength of new spirit with a hydrometer.

Left, the still room in a modern distillery. The wash still (centre, with the larger neck) produces 'low wines'; these are distilled once more, in the low wines still, to produce whisky.

alcohol, not unlike beer, which is known as 'wash', and it is from this that the distiller will finally produce the spirit which is to become Scotch whisky.

Distillation is carried out in the traditional pot stills made of copper, the shape of which has not changed since Scotch whisky was first made. The process is easy to follow. After it has been charged into the still the wash is heated to the point at which it becomes vapour. The vapour rises up the still and is then cooled so that it condenses; this separates the alcohol from the fermented liquid and what is left of the yeast and un-fermented matter. In the making of malt whisky this alcohol, known as 'low wines', is collected and distilled a second time in another still. The first and last runnings of spirit from this second distillation are known as 'foreshots' and 'feints' and are not of the quality and purity expected in Scotch whisky. Thus only the middle 'cut' of the distillation is collected, and is run into a vat called a 'spirit receiver'. The foreshots or feints are returned to the still, charged again with low wines and re-distilled.

As soon as any form of alcohol is produced in a distil-lery, the entire process passes under the inspection of the Customs and Excise. The amounts of wash, low wines and spirit are carefully checked and recorded so that in due course the appropriate amount of Excise Duty can be assessed and collected. This means that all the equipment used in a distillery from the process of fermentation onwards is kept locked. The spirit flowing from the stills passes through the spirit safe; this is a form of glass case and such tests as the stillman may wish to make must be carried out by remote control. Nevertheless, it is the stillman who decides when the spirit is of the quality required and may be collected, and in making this judgment he must rely to a large extent on skills that can only be acquired by experience.

Grain Whisky differs from malt whisky both in the method by which it is distilled and in the cereals used. The patent still provides continuous distillation and can therefore produce whisky in much larger quantities than the batch operation of pot stills. And while only malted barley is used in the production of malt whisky, for grain whisky both malted barley and unmalted cereals, usually maize, are the basic raw materials.

Before mashing, the unmalted cereals are cooked by steam pressure in converters. The starch cells in the grain burst, and when this liquid is mixed in the mash tun with malted barley the enzymes in the latter con-vert this starch into a form of sugar. Although the fermentation of the worts in wash-backs is the same as

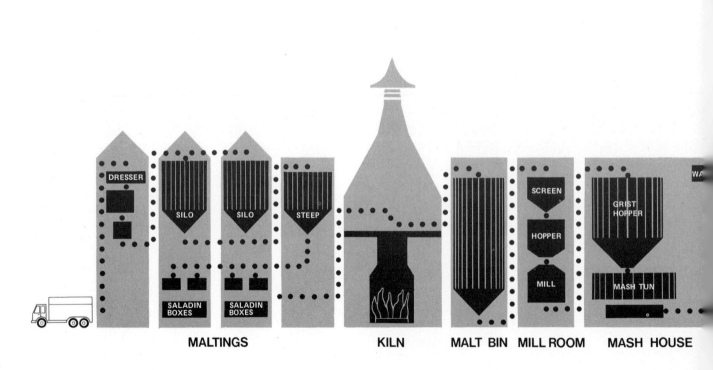

MALTINGS   KILN   MALT BIN   MILL ROOM   MASH HOUSE

Diagram from a late-nineteenth-century advertisement for a manufacturer of 'every description of Distillery and Brewery Plant'.

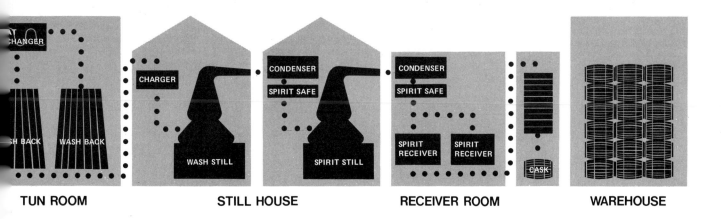

TUN ROOM   **STILL HOUSE**   **RECEIVER ROOM**   **WAREHOUSE**

Maize, one of the cereals from which grain whisky is made.

In majestic hoppers such as this, maize is stored until required for use.

Here, in the mash tun, the unmalted cereals are mixed with malted barley and hot water. As with malt whisky, mashing produces a sugary liquid ready for fermentation.

Two views of the control panel of a patent still: although modern technology has its place in the distillery, in the last analysis quality is dependent upon the judgment of the individual stillman.

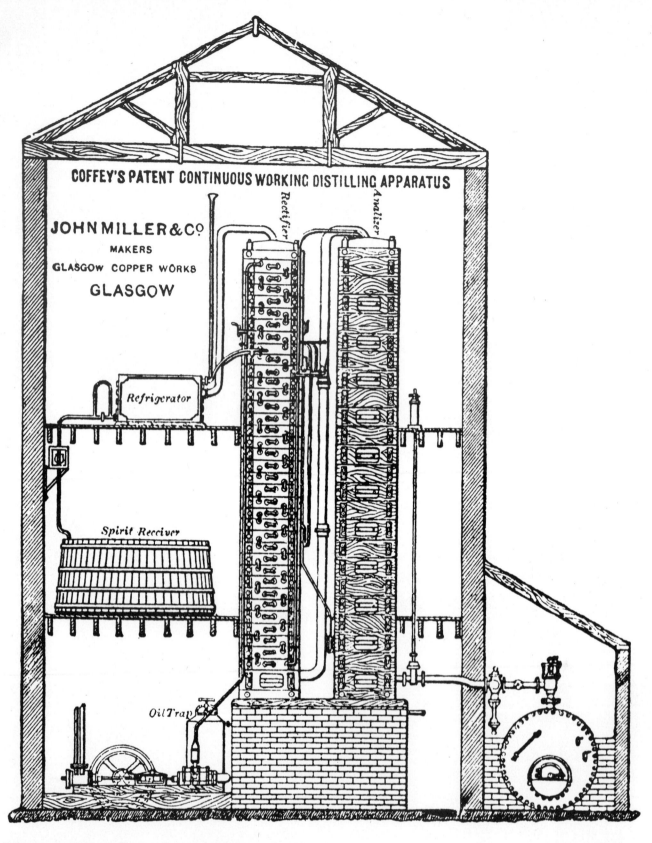

Diagram of a Coffey Still, part of an advertisement produced by John Miller & Company of Glasgow, c. 1897.

for malt whisky, the process of distillation is very different.

The patent still consists of two tall columns, one called the analyser and the other the rectifier, both of which are divided horizontally into a series of chambers. Steam is charged into the base of the analyser, and when both columns are full of steam, the wash is fed into the top of the rectifier. As it passes in a pipe down the rectifier, it is heated by the rising steam almost to boiling-point, after which it is carried to the top of the analyser. In the analyser the wash moves down through the series of chambers, and as it moves the alcohol in it is vaporised by the rising steam. The vapours mixed with steam are then fed into the base of the rectifier where, as they ascend, they are cooled by the descending wash. Eventually the alcohol condenses into spirit and is collected.

Because of the cereals used in its production and because it is distilled at higher strength, grain whisky is lighter in flavour and character than malt whisky. It is nevertheless a true whisky which draws its flavour and aroma solely from the materials used. This is worth emphasising because in some parts of the world there are those who like to claim, for their own purposes, that it is a neutral spirit. It is perfectly possible to produce neutral spirit in a patent still, but the law defining Scotch whisky lays down the maximum strength at which it may be distilled, and it is above this point that the spirit would begin to lose flavour very rapidly. The difference between grain whisky and neutral spirit can easily be discerned by either taste or smell. Before the practice of blending began, large quantities of grain whisky were bottled and sold as 'single' whiskies, and a small demand continues to exist among those who prefer it to either malt or blended whisky.

The spirit which emerges from either the pot still or the patent still is not yet whisky and cannot by law be described as such. Before qualifying for this description the spirit must be allowed to mature for a period of at least three years. The way in which this maturation takes place is one of the most fascinating aspects in the making of Scotch whisky and one about which still comparatively little is known. Anyone who has had the opportunity of tasting a glass of new spirit straight from the still and comparing it with matured whisky can only be astonished at how a coarse and not particularly palatable spirit becomes a smooth, mellow and satisfying drink. And yet this transformation is effected simply by allowing the spirit to lie in a

Drawing off grain whisky through a spirit receiver.

A cooper's workshop. The skills of the coopers, who make and maintain the casks, play a crucial role in the manufacture of whisky.

Opposite, maturing whisky in the warehouse: here casks will be stored for a minimum of three years, perhaps for as many as fifteen or even longer.

Filling casks with newly distilled spirit and, right, rolling a cask to the position where it will be left to mature.

cask made from oak. Nothing is added and no form of treatment is given. Maturation is a wholly natural process and one which only time can achieve.

All one can say with any certainty is that certain undesirable constituents in the whisky are removed by chemical changes resulting from oxidisation and that for these to take place there must be a slow evaporation of the whisky. It follows that the casks in which the whisky matures must be permeable to allow the air to reach the whisky, and long experience has shown that casks made from oak are the most suitable. At one time casks that had formerly contained sherry were mainly used, and these give the whisky a darker colour and a slightly sweetish flavour. Today a large proportion of casks is imported from the United States after being used there for American whisky. The casks arrive broken down in bundles of staves and are reassembled in the distillery cooperage, where repairs may also be carried out. When casks made from new wood are used they must first be treated before being filled.

The rate at which whisky matures is influenced by both the type and the size of casks in which it is filled: as a normal rule, the smaller the cask the faster the maturation. Other features that must be taken into account are the temperature and humidity of the warehouse in which the casks are stored. In general grain whiskies and the lighter lowland malt whiskies mature more quickly than Highland or Islay malts. Although by law Scotch whisky need only be matured for three years, for standard brands an average of four to six years is normal, while de luxe and single malt whiskies are often left to mature for twelve, fifteen or even twenty years. There is a danger, however, that after fifteen years the whisky may take on a flavour of woodiness from the cask and be spoiled.

Throughout the period when it is maturing, Scotch whisky requires little attention. For years the casks can be left to lie in the cool darkness of the warehouse with no more than an occasional inspection to make sure that they are not leaking. And yet maturation is probably the most costly part of the process of making whisky, since vast sums of capital have to be tied up for many years. Countless attempts have been made to find an alternative to maturation, some method of treating the new spirit that would have the same effect as those long years of waiting. They have proved only that in the making of Scotch whisky there is no substitute for time; just as all the elements which give Scotch whisky its unique flavour and character – water, peat, barley – have their origin in the slow passage of years, so it will always need the skill and patience of man to extract that flavour from those elements and bring it slowly to perfection.

A cooper reassembles a cask.

Charring a cask after inserting new staves in a cask previously used for Bourbon.

Late-nineteenth-century print showing whisky being filled into casks.

Merely by tapping a barrel, the warehouseman can tell if there has been any loss caused by leakage.

Chapter 5

Great Malt Whiskies

Hugh MacDiarmid

Being old enough (at 82!) and having been a consistent whisky drinker for about sixty years (seldom indeed having any other drink, though when abroad I might sample vodka, acquavita, slivovitz, mastika and others), I am in a position to appreciate the increase in the last few years of the availability and popularity of malt whiskies. Naturally anything I say on this is a matter of personal preference and must not be taken to imply any disparagement of the many splendid blended whiskies on the market today. And I must be careful in another respect, since I cannot claim to have tasted all the available malt whiskies, and I know that the other day on the B.B.C. television my friend Mr Magnus Magnusson told the world how just now at Mulben, in a valley just outside Keith, Mr Ivey Shaw has a spring of mountain waters, £4½ million, and a legacy which spans two generations of malt whisky making. His job this year is to create another great whisky – a Speyside Scotch, the 115th of the line.

Only a few years ago it would have been useless to ask for a malt whisky in most of the English bars and even in Scotland, south of the Highland Line. Quite recently it has become a very different story. I had occasion recently to do a lot of motoring in the Upper Tyne valley, and in all the little pubs I visited, patronised only by a few shepherds and gamekeepers outside a little tourist traffic in the season, I found that every one stocked malt whiskies, and not just one of them but several, so that customers could choose which one they wanted.

Even more surprising to me was the bar in the Students' Union of a north English university, where I found between thirty and forty malts available.

The characteristic flavour and aroma of any blend derive from the malt whiskies in it. Each of the Highland malt distilleries – there are nearly a hundred of them – produces a whisky with its own distinctive character. The differences between them have never been adequately explained and seem to depend on a variety of factors. These range from the quality of the ingredients used to the very air of the glen in which the distillery is situated, and from the exact shape of the pot still to the skill of the individual distiller. Some magical combination of the kind must be responsible for the subtle difference between the malt whiskies produced in Grant's distilleries at Glenfiddich and Balvenie, since these two distilleries are only a stone's throw apart. Yet although each is fed by the same spring of water, and each uses the same materials and the same processes, the two distilleries produce malt whiskies of subtly different character.

The increased popularity of malt whiskies in recent years carries with it a discrimination which is a good thing in itself. While malt whisky has not produced connoisseurs like the wine experts or oenophilists, most malt whisky drinkers ask by name for their preference, and I know in my own case that if I were blindfolded and given a succession of, say, ten of the best malt whiskies to sip, I could hardly fail to name each of them correctly.

It has been claimed that the flavours of the malt whiskies arise from the peculiarities of the barley

The burn at Tomatin where some three million gallons of malt whisky are distilled each year; though a single malt is produced, almost the entire production is sold for blending.

used for preparing the malt for whisky production, the superlative quality of the burn water employed for mashing the malt, and the particular geology of the area in which the most famous distilleries are located. But the distilleries are now to be found all over Scotland and the factors just mentioned vary from place to place. It is a noteworthy fact, however, that the chief centres of illicit whisky production in the old days became, and still are, the sites of the established distilleries after the Act of 1823 which enabled licensed distillers to produce spirit of a strength equal to that made by the smugglers on payment of a reasonable duty – and that pretty well put an end to the old freebooting. The rate in 1823 stood at the modest figure of 2s. 3d. per proof gallon, while the present levy is 210s. 10d. per proof gallon.

With all the great changes in economic circumstances, scientific developments and social customs, it is undoubtedly true that whisky, an uncomplicated drink to make, is at least as much about people as places or pot stills. While there are stocks of malt whisky enough to float all the world's navies there is little danger of the supply running out. None the less, the rise in world cereal prices is a matter of concern. The price of barley, the malt whisky base, has more than doubled in recent years to over £50, and the chairman of one big whisky firm has foreseen that price doubling in the near future. Barley at £100 a ton would affect the price of whisky sold in the next four or five years onwards.

Bruichladdich distillery, Islay, seen from the sea.

Discharging whisky casks at Caol Ila Distillery, Islay.

66

The Highland Park distillery at Kirkwall as it was at the end of the nineteenth century, and, below, unloading coal for the distillery in the 1920s.

While distilleries are increasing in number and size and a much greater volume of production is planned, there is no fear that the demand will fall off or that the total quantity produced will have any difficulty in finding sale. The trade is indeed in an extremely buoyant and optimistic state. Nevertheless vigilant regard must always be maintained, and an European Economic Community declaration that, owing to peat, Scottish Highland water is 'dirty' might well affect the whisky trade in foreign countries, if not in Scotland itself. There it is well known that the peat, burned in the furnaces over which the malting barley is dried, is vitally important to the whisky, as is the air in which the whisky lies for long years as it matures.

The late Mr Maurice Walsh, the novelist, has said: 'I know one small town with seven distilleries, and I know an expert who could distinguish the seven by bouquet alone. These seven distilleries were on one mile of a highland river. They used the same water, peat, and malt, and the methods of brewing and distillation were identical, yet each spirit had its own individual bouquet. One, the best, mellowed perfectly in seven years; another, the least good, was still liquid fire at the end of ten years.' Malt whiskies may be bland or 'have a kick' and it is impossible to account for the differences by any reference to the particular Highland, Island or Lowland site where they are made. One should indeed be grateful for this variety, appealing to diverse tastes, and in the last analysis the solution is most probably in the human factor. It has been well said that 'The production of whisky is undoubtedly an art, and all attempts to produce whisky by a "scientific" approach have proved to be futile. We have some scientific understanding of the processes involved in making good whisky, yet why Scottish whisky has a characteristic and unique flavour is a complete mystery. Nobody has been able to reproduce it outside Scotland.' But not for want of trying! All the imitators have failed, however, even with the blends – and they have no chance whatever to emulate and exploit the rare individual qualities of the malts.

Mortlach distillery, Dufftown.

Group of workers at Cardow distillery on Speyside, 1920.

68

Malt whiskies may be grouped into six classes and, so far as I am concerned, the roll-call of the great malts runs as follows:

The *Glenlivets* and their like, among them Macallan, Cardhu, Glenfarclas-Glenlivet, Longmorn-Glenlivet, Linkwood, Tomatin and Glen Mhor.

The *Dufftown* and nearby malts, namely the Dufftown-Glenlivet, Glenfiddich and Balvenie, Mortlach, and Auld Aultmore.

The *northern malts*, which include Old Pulteney, Clynelish and Glenmorangie.

The *Lowland malts*, particularly Bladnoch.

The *Campbeltown malts*, especially Springbank.

The *Island malts*, namely Laphroaig, Bruichladdich, Talisker and Highland Park.

I have little patience with the pseudo-poetical attempts to describe the differences in flavour of the various malts. It was once explained to me by a lover of Laphroaig, an Islay malt that rolls on you like a sea haar: 'Scottish whiskies are like an orchestra. The Islay malts are heavy and sombre as 'cellos. Highland malts are violas, Lowland the discursive violin, and grains are like pianos – sometimes *fortissimo*, sometimes *pianissimo*.' – Glenfiddich, the world's best-selling malt, may be called cream-smooth; Glenmorangie said to have a honey-sweet flavour; Talisker to be 'powerful enough to suit any man's moods – if treated with

Glenkinchie distillery: top, as it was at the end of the last century, and, beneath, a contemporary view.

Late nineteenth-century print of spirit stills in a malt whisky distillery.

wary respect' – but all such efforts are futile. You can only know any or all of them by actually drinking them.

And which is the best? I have my own preference, but if that is not available I am content enough with any of the others on that wonderful list.

When I say that finally the differences between the malts are only explicable in terms of the human factor, I cannot forget that most of these great whiskies were, and generally still are, small family concerns, with a great deal of loyalty and skill among their work people. The same families have contributed to the working forces for generations and this must have a great deal to do with the matter. It is significant, too, that while the old heroic days of smuggling, and illicit distilling, have almost entirely gone, the chief centres of illicit whisky production became, and still are, the sites for the established distilleries, so the 'know how' may well have been transmitted down the generations from the remote past, and it has certainly lost nothing in the course of time.

The great escalation and increased popularity of malt whiskies in recent years may be illustrated by the fact that one malt whisky distillery raised its output from four thousand gallons per week in 1950 to forty thousand gallons per week in 1966, while its warehouses hold over one million proof gallons of whisky –

Distillery wedding at Tomatin, c. 1910. Above, the bride; below, four of the guests. A journalist reported: 'After the ceremony, Pipe-Major Mackie played the happy couple and the guests to the malt barn, where luncheon was purveyed.'

figures typical of many malt whisky distilleries' bonded stores.

Dr J. S. McDowall has pointed out in his book *The Whiskies of Scotland* that

there are about 100 malt distilleries in operation, but more are under construction. Less than thirty of their whiskies are available to the public in bottle. Most are wholly taken up by the blenders and now there are about two thousand registered blends; indeed, when most people talk of whisky they refer to a blend. The single malt whiskies are not always easily available and are a few shillings more expensive than standard blends because of the longer time needed for them to mature. . . . In 1930 Mr Aeneas MacDonald gave the names of what he considered the thirteen best whiskies, but this must be considered quite unfair for there are several unmentioned whiskies such as Mortlach, Strathisla and GlenMhor, which today are certainly quite as good. It may be that the better known whiskies have rested a bit on their laurels and that some lesser-known ones have caught up.

Of the Glenlivets only seven have survived to appear now as single malts. Most are used for blending only.

I agree with Dr McDowall that in its heyday Bladnoch, the Lowland malt, was a very good whisky with a wonderful bouquet, but the old mature whisky is no longer available except very privately. Bruichladdich whisky is available only to local (Islay) publicans, and there are quite a number of other excellent malt whiskies which are similarly obtainable only within a very restricted range or can be had (like the best Bladnoch) only 'very privately'.

My friend the late Neil Gunn, the novelist, used to say that 'until a man has the luck to chance on a perfectly matured malt, he does not really know what whisky is'.

Whatever developments the next few years may bring, all that matters is that the quality and distinctive characteristics of Scotch should be maintained. If that is so, all is well.

Wash and low wines stills in a malt whisky distillery towards the end of the last century.

Chapter 6

The Blender's Art

Donald Mackinlay

production director, Charles Mackinlay and Company Ltd

It is on blended whisky that the international popularity and reputation of Scotch has been built. If the practice of blending Scotch whisky had never begun, the whisky trade in Scotland might not have developed beyond a cottage industry.

It was Andrew Usher who first started blending different malt whiskies in the early 1860s. After 1853, the Customs and Excise permitted the duty-paid 'vatting' of whiskies from the same distillery, but of different years, and after 1860 the blending in bond of whiskies from different distilleries. Both operations were designed so that a product of consistent quality could be guaranteed. It was not therefore a large step for him to take grain whisky, which up to this time, like the malts, had been sold as an individual product, and blend both grain and malt.

It is probably true to say that the early blends first found acceptance in the London market because they had a somewhat lighter character than the malt whisky which had been available until that time. It is also interesting to note that according to the anonymous author of *London in the Sixties* whisky at this period was literally an unknown beverage in London, possibly because the supply could never have equalled the demand. Sir Winston Churchill recorded that his father 'never drank whisky, except on a moor or in some very dull and chilly place'.

These early blends laid the foundation for the great brands that developed towards the end of the nineteenth and at the beginning of the twentieth centuries. The proprietor of a blend would guard jealously the particular secret of his brand. Its individuality could well have stemmed either from his ownership of a malt distillery or from his strong connections with one of the many malt distilleries. During the evolution of

View of Messrs. Andrew Usher and Co's bonded warehouse at Edinburgh, c. 1897. The store had a total capacity of some fifteen thousand casks.

Nosing a sample of whisky. A blender will test a row of whiskies such as this in some ten minutes, quickly and carefully checking that each element of his blend has matured fully and is not contaminated in any way.

Transporting whisky from distillery to railway station for dispatch to the blender.

blends as we know them today the number of distilleries in Scotland producing whisky has decreased from 167 in 1902 to some 120 in 1974. The reason for this is that certain distilleries were not favoured by the blenders for blending purposes, and if their production had no sale as a straight malt they had no option but to close down.

There are many reasons why Scotch whisky is blended. The most important is to produce a branded whisky that is consistent in flavour and quality at all times. If a brand of Scotch is to be marketed throughout the world on a vast scale, then it is essential that the whisky in every bottle is recognisably the same in taste and quality, no matter whether it is bought in Riga or Rio de Janeiro, in Singapore or Seattle. Moreover, the product of a single distillery could not possibly meet such massive demand. It must be versatile, appreciated both in cold and in tropical climates, as an aperitif or a liqueur or as a long drink in thirsty weather. It must at the same time be a blend with a distinctive taste and character of its own that will attract and keep the loyalty of whisky drinkers.

The art of producing a good blend of Scotch requires skill and experience. A blend will be made up of anything from twenty to fifty different whiskies carefully chosen from the 120-odd distilleries in Scotland. Haphazard selection is not enough. Whiskies, like people,

have pronounced characteristics of their own, and choosing whiskies for a blend is not unlike choosing guests for a dinner party. There are some which clash with each other, producing a discordant result, while others enhance one another, bringing out their best qualities to advantage.

By the same token there are some whiskies which, taken 'straight', have little to commend them, but added to a blend they supply some indefinable characteristic which helps to balance the other whiskies and produce a harmonious whole. These good blending whiskies are of inestimable value to the Scotch whisky trade.

To appreciate the difficulties of blending, the layman should experiment on his own account. He may take half a dozen of the finest highland malts, those from the classic distilleries, mix them together and add any proportion he chooses of grain whisky. The result will almost certainly be a blend that is totally unacceptable, one in which all the subtle distinctive qualities of the different malts have been entirely lost. The truth is that a good blend requires whiskies of less pronounced character just as much as it needs the classic malts.

In other words, the art of blending is not to mix good with less good and produce a mediocre but inoffensive whisky. On the contrary, the objective is to make a blend that draws the best qualities from all its component whiskies, one which has flavour and character in its own right.

There are no set rules to guide the blender in making up his formula. One cannot say that a blend containing 45 per cent malt is any better than one which contains only 35 per cent. Generally speaking an older blend, say a twelve-year-old, needs a higher proportion of malt than a six-year-old. Similarly, age is not always synonymous with quality.

The age claimed for a blended whisky must by law be that of the youngest whisky in the blend. It is not permissible to give an average age. If therefore a company wishes to market a twelve-year-old blend and sell it as such, all the component whiskies must be allowed to mature for at least twelve years.

Having settled on the formula for its blend, the blending company must buy the necessary quantities of new whisky from the different distilleries and allow it to mature. The custom of the trade is that the

Drawing samples in a modern blending hall: here whiskies used in a blend are emptied into troughs to flow to the blending vats.

Unloading barrels of Islay malt en route from the distillery to the blender. At this stage duty has not been paid on the whisky in the cask, but tests are made on arrival to ensure that whisky has not been extracted from the cask during the journey.

Drawing a sample of whisky for the blender to nose.

Once accepted by the blender, all the individual malt and grain whiskies for the entire blend are emptied into a blending trough, from where the whisky flows to the blending vats.

Blending vats. Here the whisky is roused for a brief period and then left for two or three days before being drawn off into wood again for a period of 'marrying'.

Filling casks with whisky from the blending vats.

In these casks the whisky is left for at least six months, or even a year, to allow the different components of the blend to 'marry'.

Some of the many whiskies that make up a blend. Whisky is a clear spirit and takes its colour from the type of cask in which it matures – a refilled cask will impart little colour, a sherry cask will produce a dark whisky.

blending company buys new whisky as 'fillings' and provides the casks to be filled. The whisky is then allowed to mature in the distillery warehouses until, in the opinion of the blender, it is ready to be added to his blend.

Now the skill and experience of the blender come into play. When each cask of whisky approaches the appropriate age, a sample is drawn and sent to the sampling room. It is then the responsibility of the blender to accept it as suitable for inclusion in the company's blend.

Whisky blenders work by their sense of smell alone. A little whisky from the sample is poured into a tulip-shaped glass, water is added and the glass well shaken before the whisky is smelt or 'nosed'. The addition of water releases the full aroma of the whisky and reduces it to the correct strength for sampling. Provided his nose tells him that everything is all right, the blender can accept the sample.

In all but the smallest companies there will be more than one blender on the staff. In doubtful cases, therefore, a blender may get a second opinion on a sample from a colleague. This is a great advantage in work that is solely a question of judgment and where differences in smell can be infinitesimal.

The sample room in a whisky company may lack the romance of a malt kiln or a still room, but it has a fascination of its own.

A blender may have to 'nose' as many as 750 samples in a day. This is exacting work demanding a high degree of concentration, and normally he will not nose more than seventy or eighty samples before taking a break.

The sample room is usually a quiet place where noise and distractions are kept to a minimum. Alien smells must also be excluded. For this reason many blenders ban women from entering their sample room, not through misogyny, but because they may be wearing perfume. It is rare that a blender ever tastes whisky while he is at work, because the taste of a particular whisky may affect his ability to nose the subsequent samples.

To be run efficiently in today's competitive conditions, a blending company must have adequate stocks of whisky maturing to produce its various blends, in sufficient quantity to meet all foreseeable demand. Deficiencies of certain whiskies can be made up by exchange with other companies or by buying mature whisky through a broker, but this is a recourse in emergencies only.

The role of the blender in a whisky company is becoming increasingly important as the scale of operation grows ever larger to meet world demand. An

error of judgment in accepting a sample from a single cask could result in the production of a faulty blend of several thousand gallons.

After the various casks of whisky have been passed by the blender, they are poured, in the correct proportion, into a blending trough through which they pass into the blending vat. In these vessels, which may hold as much as 25,000 gallons, the whisky is thoroughly 'roused' or mixed by compressed air. The blend is then poured back into casks and stored for a further period, usually for six months but sometimes for as

long as a year. The object is to allow the different whiskies to 'marry' and become intimately mixed in the final blend. This again is an expensive business, since it means keeping valuable stocks of mature whisky lying idle, but experience has shown that it is essential if a blended whisky of quality is to be produced.

It is at this stage that water is added to reduce the blend to the required strength. The water used is as vital as it is in the initial distillation, and once again the soft water of Scotland comes to the fore and helps to complete the process. It is also necessary to add a small proportion of colour to ensure that the colour of the whisky in the bottle is always the same. This quantity is so small that it in no way affects the quality, taste or bouquet of the whisky. Finally, the blended whisky is filtered and then bottled, labelled and packed in cases, ready for sale.

Nowadays bottling is done by automatic machinery, the only way of keeping pace with the growing demand for Scotch whisky. A modern bottling hall will have several bottling lines operating at speed and filling all

A modern bottling hall, where several bottling lines operate simultaneously and the same scene at the end of the last century.

Before bottling, a sample is taken and its colour is checked to ensure that the uniform colour of the brand is maintained.

An automatic filling machine in a modern bottling hall.

After being filled, each bottle is carefully inspected to ensure a perfect presentation before it is packed for dispatch.

Ready for consumption, the whisky sets out on its journey to the customer – perhaps a few miles away or across half the world.

the many different sizes of bottle that are required for different markets. Although the process is almost entirely automatic, careful supervision is essential and every bottle is examined before it is labelled and packed.

Late-nineteenth-century photograph of whisky being loaded for export.

The tremendous increase in the export of whisky has been made possible by production increases at the individual malt distilleries that were undreamt of in the early 1900s. These increases have all been carried out with the greatest care to ensure that the character of the whisky produced is not altered. The closure of distilleries during the early part of the century has also been compensated for by the construction of some completely new distilleries in the 1960s and 1970s. Certainly those built during the 1960s are now beginning to take their place in some of the blends being sold in world markets. This is where the art of the blender really comes into its own. Once they have matured, he must make use of these newcomers to the malt scene without altering the character of his blend. This is achieved by subtly re-arranging the quantities of different malts and grains used in the blend.

The job of the blender has not changed through the ages, and his most valued possession is still his sense of smell. This will tell him the age of whisky, the area from which it comes and indeed the distillery. No instrument has yet been produced to carry out this function, and thus the art of blending remains virtually untouched by modern methods of analysis.

Export breakthrough! The first consignment of Teacher's Whisky sold to the USA.

Chapter 7

In Praise of Famous Names

Jack House

According to the law of Scotland (which is quite a different as from the law of England) you are not allowed to make water in public or whisky in private! The second part of this edict means that it is sometimes difficult to determine the year when a well known whisky was first made. There are one or two famous whiskies for which the claim is made that they go back at least to the eighteenth century. This is very difficult to prove – or to disprove, for that matter.

Now, however, the really famous names are all blends, and their fame rests in part on the men who brought as many as forty whiskies – Highland malt, Islay malt, Lowland malt and grain – together and achieved that fine smooth strength which characterises a good whisky, and at least equally on the men who promoted these blends, the entrepreneurs, the salesmen, the business experts.

There will always be arguments about whether or not the single whisky is better than the blend. More to the point is the fact that, if the blenders had not developed their magic touch, whisky might not have become the most popular drink in the world.

Take the blenders first, for the businessmen could have done nothing without the blends. There will always be arguments about the identity of the first Scotch whisky blender. For a long time both Glasgow and Edinburgh claimed him – yet it is possible that blending was being tried in other parts of Scotland as well. Edinburgh maintained that Andrew Usher (who eventually made so much money out of whisky that he

Advertisement issued in 1893 for Scotland's 'choicest product' by John Robertson and Son.

gave the capital city the hall named after him) was the first man to blend whiskies successfully. Glasgow said it was a wine merchant named W. P. Lowrie – the man who could fairly be said to have given the amazing James Buchanan (Black & White) his start.

On the whole, the balance comes down on the side of Edinburgh. Andrew Usher dealt with the Glenlivet distilleries and in 1853 he had the idea of mixing the old pot-still malts with the comparatively new patent-still grain whisky. At about the same time Lowrie was carrying out blending experiments in Glasgow. And history supports Usher's claim, for a blend known as Usher's Green Stripe is still sold today. There is, of course, a story that John Dewar, the man who started Dewar's of Perth (White Label) accidentally stumbled upon a blend by mixing the remains of whisky in almost empty casks. This appears to be just a story, although it is true that one of Scotland's greatest whisky blenders was John Alexander Cameron, who first 'made' White Label whisky.

Though I have allowed Edinburgh to claim the first whisky blender, I should really have said Leith, for Leith was a separate town in those days. Indeed, Leith could fairly claim to have been the Scotch whisky centre of the world at one time. One of the great blenders there was William Sanderson, who started as a wine and cordial manufacturer but became more and more interested in whisky. He invented a drink called 'Aqua Shrub', which was a mixture of whisky,

Andrew Usher, the first of a long line of successful whisky blenders.

83

fruit juice and sugar, and also brought out 'Whisky Bitters', which was an infusion of aromatic herbs and whisky.

William Sanderson and his son, William Mark, were among the first merchants to put whisky into bottles (which were made locally in Leith) instead of selling the stuff by the cask or keg. It was William Mark who made this successful suggestion to his father and he then persuaded him to finalise his experiments and produce a definite blend which could be put on the market.

So, in July 1882, William Sanderson made up close on a hundred different blends, experimenting with differing amounts of malt and grain whiskies in each of them. The various whiskies were put into small, numbered casks, and William then invited some blenders, along with some of his friends who had a fine taste for whisky, to a whisky-tasting. They were unanimous that the best blend was vatting number 69, and so Vat 69 whisky was born. Incidentally, it was William Sanderson's choice too.

It did not take long for Vat 69 to become popular, and today the brand is still made from the same recipe

William Sanderson.

picked out as the best by William Sanderson and his friends many years ago.

One of William Sanderson's friends was John Begg, who built Lochnagar distillery only a mile or so from Balmoral Castle. Quite a lot of Lochnagar malt was used in Vat 69, although 'Take a peg of John Begg' has been a well-known whisky slogan for years. David Daiches says that it is the only whisky he knows which has had its slogan translated into Yiddish. In a Glasgow Jewish newspaper it appeared as 'Nem a schmeck fun Dzon Bek'!

The Begg distillery is now the Royal Lochnagar. The reason for this distinction goes back to a day in 1848 when Queen Victoria and Prince Albert were at Balmoral. The enterprising Mr Begg sent a note to the Castle to let Prince Albert know that the distillery was now in full operation. The royal party lost no time. They received the note at 9 p.m. and arrived at the distillery without delay, at 4 p.m. the following day. 'We have come to see through your works', said Prince Albert.

In his diary Mr Begg noted:

I endeavoured to explain the whole process of malting, brewing and distilling, showing the Royal Party the barley in its original state, and in all its different stages of manufacture until it came out of the still pipe in spirits. H.R.H. tasted the spirits with his fingers from both the still pipes. On going downstairs H.R.H. turned to me and said (looking at the locks on the stills), 'I see you have got your locks there.' On my replying, 'These are the Queen's locks', Her Majesty took a hearty laugh.

When we came to the door I asked H.R.H. if he would like to taste the spirit in its matured state, as we had cleared some that day from bond, which I thought was very fine. H.R.H. having agreed to this, I called for a bottle and glasses (which had been previously in readiness) and, presenting one glass to Her Majesty, she tasted it. So also did His Royal Highness the Prince. I then presented a glass to the Princess Royal, and to the Prince of Wales, and Prince Alfred, all of whom tasted the spirit.

H.R.H. the Prince of Wales was going to carry his glass quickly to his mouth. I checked him, saying it was very strong, so he did not take but a very small drop of it. Afterwards the Royal Party took their departure.

The next thing that happened to John Begg was that he was appointed distiller to the Queen by royal warrant – so maybe John Begg was a whisky promoter as well as a whisky blender!

It is a far cry though from Lochnagar to the pushing methods which the whisky entrepreneurs used during the great whisky boom towards the end of the last century. Outstanding among these men were the

Nineteenth-century advertisement for Pattisons' whisky, reflecting Britain's imperial fervour.

IN "GENERAL" USE.

A Commanding Spirit finds its way to the front. PATTISONS' WHISKY commands success because it has been found by the public to be a genuine, wholesome, palatable beverage, carefully blended and thoroughly matured. It is cream-like in taste, with all the stimulating qualities of the pure Highland spirit. Sold Here, There, and Everywhere.

Sole Proprietors: **PATTISONS, Ltd., Highland Distillers, BALLINDALLOCH, LEITH, and LONDON.**
Head Offices: CONSTITUTION STREET, LEITH.

Pattison brothers, Robert and Walter. They were running a successful wholesale grocery business in Leith when they decided to go into whisky. They believed in advertising, and their posters were forceful when posters were still expected to be fairly sedate. They sent hundreds of grey parrots all over the country, each trained to squawk 'Drink Pattison's whisky!' Every licensed grocer of any note in Scotland had a Pattison parrot.

The Pattison brothers became a limited company and people rushed to buy shares. They built a mansion in the Leith Walk. Robert obviously suffered from *folies de grandeur* because one of his occasional habits was to miss the train to Edinburgh when he was returning from his country estate near Peebles. Then he would order a private train at the cost of £5 1s. a mile. He thought the resulting publicity well worth it.

The Pattisons over-reached themselves. They went bust in December 1898, were tried for fraud, and Robert was sent to prison for eighteen months and Walter for eight months.

Let me turn to happier things – to the stories of those known in the whisky business as 'the Big Five'.

The famous names are Haig, Dewar, Buchanan, Walker and Mackie, and the oldest name of that Scotch quintet was not originally Scottish at all. The Haigs were Normans by the name of de la Hage. The first Haig to go into the whisky business was Robert, who, in January 1665, appeared before the Kirk Session of St Ninian's Parish Church in Stirlingshire, charged with Sabbath breaking because he allowed distilling to take place on a Sunday.

The Haigs learnt their distilling not from the Highlands but from Holland and were linked with the Stein family, who owned distilleries in Clackmannanshire. They too had Dutch connections. A Haig girl married John Jameson, and they went to Ireland and founded the Irish whiskey firm of John Jameson and Son in Dublin. The most famous director of the firm is, of course, the commander-in-chief of the British Forces in the First World War, Lord Haig himself.

To avoid confusion, I should explain that Haig and Haig in the United States is the same as plain Haig in the United Kingdom. And you may be interested to know that the whisky which disappeared from the ship wrecked off the Isle of Eriskay during the Second

Advertisement dating from about 1900 for Uam-Var whisky.

Field-Marshal Earl Haig, commander-in-chief of the British forces in the First World War and one of the original directors of John Haig and Company.

World War was Haig and Haig. Sir Compton Mackenzie made the story into his famous novel *Whisky Galore*. The film of that book had even greater success, as *Whisky Galore* in Britain, *Tight Little Island* in the United States and *Whisky à Gogo* in Europe.

Probably the first real whisky entrepreneur was the immensely popular Tommy Dewar. He was one of the two sons of John Dewar, who ran a small wine and spirit business in Perth. The boys were apprenticed to the business in Leith. When their father died, the elder brother, John Alexander Dewar, decided to expand the business to England and sent Thomas Robert Dewar, then barely twenty-one years old, to London to hunt out orders. Young Tommy had intro-

ductions to only two men in London: when he arrived, he found that one was dead and the other was bankrupt.

But nothing could keep Tommy Dewar down. At the Brewers' Show in the Agricultural Hall he arrived playing the bagpipes so loudly that all other sounds were drowned. The publicity was wonderful, and Tommy went on to greater things. On the old Shot Tower on the South Bank of the Thames near Waterloo Bridge he had an enormous electric sign showing a Highlander regularly raising a glass of whisky to his lips.

John Dewar stayed at home in Perth and looked after the production; Tommy travelled the world and looked after the sales. John became Baron Forteviot of Dupplin and was Lord Provost of Perth, while his

Clippers enjoying a dram of Dewar's whisky at the end of the shearing, 1867.

At least you don't
need to worry
about the quality
of your Whisky

JOHNNIE WALKER

has seen to that.

Never mind
the
Chancellor's
figures—look
at these:—

3,863,481
GALLONS

of pure malt Scotch whisky in
bond, ageing, on the date of the
last annual audit !

This vast reserve stock is your
absolute safeguard against a
single bottle of immature Johnnie
Walker. It is the bona fide
property of John Walker &
Sons, Ltd.

JOHN WALKER & SONS, LTD.,
SCOTCH WHISKY DISTILLERS,
KILMARNOCK.

Born 1820
Still going
strong

Tom Browne

brother became Baron Dewar of Homestall, Sussex, and was Sheriff of London. Tommy never married. His hobbies were horse-racing and speaking at dinners. His 'Dewarisms' were famous – one was 'Do right, and fear no man. Don't write and fear no woman.'

It's strange how many of the great Scotch whisky businesses have grown out of a single small shop. This is the case with Johnnie Walker, the world's largest selling Scotch whisky; 2½ million bottles are produced each week, for sale to two hundred countries. The original Johnnie Walker started a grocery, wine and spirit shop in Kilmarnock in 1820. At that time Kilmarnock was a thriving engineering and carpet-making centre and Englishmen and other foreigners coming to the town developed a liking for whisky. Soon they were ordering bottles of Walker's Kilmarnock whisky to be sent to them wrapped in rolls of carpet.

Alexander Walker joined his father in the firm and pioneered the whisky export business by encouraging merchant adventurers to take whisky on board their ships and sell it at the various ports of call. Soon local firms in many countries started placing orders for what became a highly acceptable drink.

It was only in 1908 that the famous Johnnie Walker red and black slanted labels and the striding figure trademark appeared, together with the slogan 'Born 1820, still going strong'. The sketch produced by the famous artist Tom Browne for Sir Alexander, was based on the original John Walker. The slogan was created by Lord Stevenson, another Kilmarnock man

who had joined Johnnie Walker, and he wrote the world-famous words across the sketch which still hangs in the company's London headquarters.

We come back to flamboyancy with James Buchanan, founder of Black & White, entrepreneur extraordinary, created Baron Woolavington, winner of the Derby and the St Leger and munificent donor to the British Museum, the Middlesex Hospital and Edinburgh University, to name but a few.

Buchanan's parents emigrated to Canada from Scotland, but shortly after he was born there they brought the baby back to Glasgow, lived in Northern Ireland for a short spell and then settled in Glasgow once again. When James left school he did a succession of office boy and clerking jobs, then found himself a post in London, acting as agent for Charles Mackinlay and Co., whisky blenders of Leith. This was in 1879. Within five years he had decided to go it alone and form his own company. In this he had the invaluable help of W. P. Lowrie, the Glasgow wine merchant who had gone into whisky as well. Lowrie gave Buchanan supplies of whisky and was ready to wait until the young man – he was only thirty-five – could pay for them.

Once James Buchanan got started, he could do no wrong. He blended his whisky from Lowrie stocks and put it into black bottles with a white label on them. This caught the eye of Londoners, who kept asking for the black and white whisky, although the actual name on the bottle was 'Buchanan's Blend'. Indeed, it was

One of the first of Tom Browne's Johnnie Walker advertisements – and its appeal remains as topical today as it was over sixty years ago.

Some of the great variety of lorries and vans used for delivering Johnnie Walker whisky in the 1920s.

under this name that he won the gold medal for blended whisky at the Paris Centennial Exhibition in 1889.

In his reminiscences James Buchanan is quite open about his methods. He courted the right people. He even courted the right girls, in a strictly business sense. He won whisky contracts for the bars of the London music halls and was the first man to supply whisky to the House of Commons. For a while 'Buchanan's Blend' had 'House of Commons' on its label in even larger letters. But the public won in the end. Whatever he called his whisky, Buchanan had to admit that people still asked for the black and white bottle, so he gave in and registered the name of Black & White.

There is a story that he took along some Scotch terriers to his advertising agency and that out of that came the advertisement with the black and white dogs. But there are so many stories about James Buchanan that you cannot tell which is true and which is, perhaps, embroidered. A favourite one relates how he had a team of young men-about-town in London. He would make certain, first of all, that a particular hotel or restaurant did not stock Black & White. Then he would send his team along one evening. They would enter the restaurant, choose a prominent table, order a magnificent meal, and then call for the wine waiter and ask for Black & White whisky.

The wine waiter would have to admit that he didn't have such a thing: whereupon the young men-about-town would rise from the table, cancel the dinner order, and walk out with cries of, 'What kind of a place is this, where you can't get Black & White!'

James Buchanan was a man who thoroughly enjoyed himself, right up until his death in 1935, at the age of nearly eighty-six. He, Tommy Dewar and Peter Mackie were typical of the Scotch whisky barons – though in fact Peter Mackie was never created a baron.

Peter Mackie, known to his contemporaries as 'Restless Peter', did become a knight, however, and was the hero of the White Horse saga. Mackie was the nephew of a Glasgow distiller, James Logan Mackie, who with his partner, Captain Graham, owned Lagavulin Distillery in Islay. They made a blend of a

James Buchanan, created Lord Woolavington, started business in 1884 with the aid of a loan; on his death in 1935 his estate was valued at over £7 million.

One of the fleet of White Horse lorries in the early 1930s.

Sir Peter Mackie.

The White Horse Inn, Edinburgh, c. 1745.

number of malts, including Lagavulin and a malt from Craigellachie, and grain whisky, and chose as its name White Horse.

Nephew Peter saw the importance of a brand name and exploited White Horse in every possible way. He linked the whisky with the White Horse Inn of Edinburgh's Royal Mile, a howff with connections with Bonnie Prince Charlie, Samuel Johnson and James Boswell. He even brought Mary Queen of Scots into the story, because she was wont to ride a white palfrey. The White Horse Inn bore the date 1742, so White Horse whisky carried the same date, although it was not actually blended until nearly 150 years later.

Apologists for the White Horse story have averred that it could go back to 1742, because there were several secret stills on the island of Islay just above where Lagavulin Distillery stands today. But the fact is that 'Restless Peter' was the man who thought up the White Horse story, authentic or not. The odd thing is that he kept saying he didn't believe in advertising!

Sir Peter Mackie loved Islay and wore Highland dress on every possible occasion. He wrote books, was strong for the Tory party, was a great Empire man,

collected old masters and antique furniture, supported cricket financially, put up the money for the Mackie Anthropological Expedition to East Africa, and even sponsored a health-giving flour called BBM (Brains, Bone and Muscle) which he commanded his employees to use.

The foundations of Queen Anne's export success, particularly in North America, were laid by another enterprising businessman, one William Shaw. The firm was already old-established when it took on this remarkable young man in the 1880s, and he climbed the company ladder rapidly as it was realised that his ability matched his ambition. Sensing the great potential of the export trade, he travelled extensively in Canada and the United States, building up business and breaking into new markets.

William Shaw established a tradition that was to be continued by his descendants. The close family association with the firm (which is now a member of the Glenlivet Distillers Limited) continues today and its Chairman, Mr W. J. Shaw, is a grandson of the original William Shaw.

There are many other famous names in the world

Stillhouse at the Nevis distillery, c. 1900.

of Scotch whisky, all worth remembering for various reasons, though lack of space means that some of them must be omitted here.

Let's start with Long John, who was a real man. He was known as Long John Macdonald, six feet four inches in height and a fine figure in his kilt. His lineage has been traced back to John Macdonald, Lord of the Isles, who wed Princess Margaret of Scotland in the fourteenth century. The Lord of the Isles regarded himself as at least the equal of the King of Scots. Our

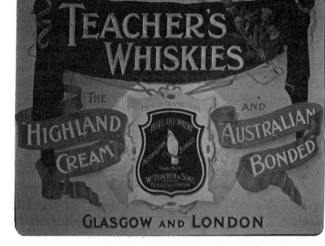

One of the first Teacher's labels.

Distillery workers, c. 1900

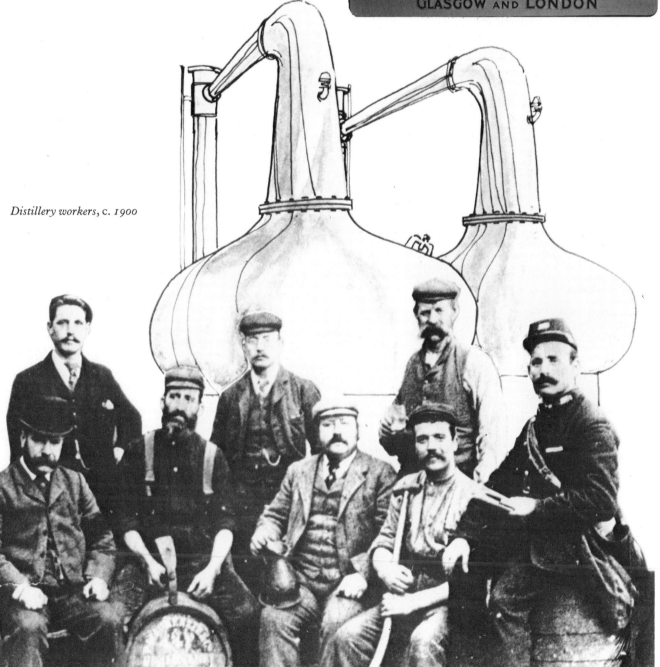

Long John, the founder of the firm, built the Ben Nevis distillery in 1825, but the name Long John now applies to a well-known brand which has no connection with that distillery.

Strange to say, there was also a man named Teacher, and he was over six feet tall too. Teacher's Highland Cream is named after William Teacher, born in 1811, who started the first of his 'dram-shops' in Glasgow when he was only nineteen. He ruled his pubs absolutely. Drunkenness and smoking were forbidden. So was 'treating', a Scottish custom where everybody in the company buys a round of drinks for everybody else. Soon William Teacher became the largest single licence-holder in Glasgow, with eighteen dram-shops. Some of his customers asked him to blend whisky to their specifications, and this led to William Teacher working out his own blend, the one on sale today.

William Grant in his uniform as a Major in the Volunteer Movement – the highest rank that could be attained by a non-professional soldier.

Late nineteenth-century advertisement for two blends sold by Henderson & Turnbull.

It's interesting to know that the favourite Scotch whisky in Scotland is Bell's. Like many other companies, Arthur Bell and Sons started in 1825, soon after distilling had been legalised. Originally the firm was merely a wines and spirits shop in the shadow of the kirk of St John in the centre of Perth. Today, Bell's 'show' distillery is the Blair Athol at Pitlochry, probably the most pleasant distillery to visit in Scotland.

I have already mentioned that great whisky, The Glenlivet. Now it is connected with another famous Speyside whisky, Glen Grant. The first Grants, John and James, were whisky smugglers in Glenlivet, though James had studied law in Edinburgh and was actually a solicitor in Elgin. He and his brother built a distillery in Rothes and then put up a new one, to exactly the same specifications, next door. The excise authorities demanded that the whisky from the new distillery should be pumped into the old distillery, and this was done through a pipe which crossed the main street and was known locally as the 'Whisky Pipe'. Although the two distilleries were structurally the same and used water from the same burn, the whiskies were entirely different.

Another Grant family is the one which produces Grant's Standfast and the single malts, Glenfiddich and Balvenie. The Grant who started the firm, William by name, had worked for some time in Mortlach distillery, the home of a notable single malt. He decided to branch out on his own and built Glenfiddich distillery, which started producing spirit in 1887. His whisky's name comes from the Clan Grant slogan, 'Stand fast, Craigellachie!' The first salesman for Standfast made five hundred calls before he was able to sell a single case, so it is told, though they've made up for that since then!

Cutty Sark Whisky, launched in 1923, was the first light-coloured whisky to be marketed; its worldwide success – it achieved brand leadership in the USA thirteen years ago – has won the Queen's Award to Industry (1971) for its manufacturers, Berry Brothers & Rudd, the well-known wine and spirit merchants. Named after the famous clipper, the whisky's link with the sea continues, for in 1972 Berry Brothers & Rudd began to sponsor the Sail Training Association's Tall Ships Race. Held every two years, this famous race unites young people of all nations·

Advertisement for Mountain Dew and Second to None, two well-known nineteenth-century blends.

95

In this panegyric of the famous names in Scotch whisky it seems odd to come across an Italian one. One of the most popular blended Scotch whiskies in the United States is J and B 'Rare'. J and B of course stands for the name of the company, Justerini and Brooks.

Why Justerini? Giacomo Justerini of Bologna was a young man in love with a beautiful opera singer, Margherita Bellino. When Margherita went to London to join the Italian Opera company there, Justerini followed her. He took with him the recipe for certain Italian liqueurs and eventually formed a partnership with Samuel Johnson – who was in fact a Cheshire dancing-master, not Boswell's Dr Johnson. The firm was known as Johnson and Justerini.

Justerini arrived in London in 1749 and had made so much money out of liqueurs and wines that he was able to retire to Italy in 1760. The Johnson family kept the firm going until 1831 when it was sold to young Alfred Brooks. For no reason that anyone can fathom, Alfred changed the name from Johnson and Justerini to Justerini and Brooks, and so it remains today.

Though J and B only entered the Scotch whisky business in the 1880s, their success has made up for their late start. They were originally only blenders but have now had their own distilleries for a number of years. In 1963 the President of the Board of Trade, the Rt Hon. Edward Heath, later to become Prime Minister, opened their new bonded warehouse at Strathleven.

Another Scotch whisky famous in America is Chivas Regal. Today this is marketed in the most modern fashion, but its history goes back to the Chivas brothers of Aberdeen who set up in business as Italian Warehousemen in 1801. They produced a blend of whisky called Chivas Regal which in those early years was a blend of twenty-five-year-old whiskies.

In 1949 Chivas Brothers was acquired with other Scotch whisky concerns by Distillers Corporation Limited of Canada, at that time under the direction of Mr Samuel Bronfman. In the following year, Strathisla Distillery, said to be the oldest operating distillery in the Highlands, was acquired by Chivas; this distillery had been in operation since 1786 and a stone in the wall bears the date 1695.

Chivas is a big firm today and owns three distilleries in the north of Scotland and modern blending and bottling plants and bonded warehouses throughout Scotland. Robert Bruce, the warrior king who gave Scotland her independence in 1314, is a key figure in the insignia of Chivas Brothers Limited, and this fact points to the personality and love of Scotland of the man who established Chivas Regal's reputation.

Chivas is not the only whisky with North American connections. Back in the 1930s, the long-established and much-respected Canadian group, Hiram Walker-Gooderman & Worts Limited, realised the enormous potential of Scotch whisky in the world's markets and consequently acquired an interest in three Scotch whisky companies. This led to the formation of Hiram Walker & Sons (Scotland) Limited and the creation of a distillery complex at Dumbarton, completed in 1938. Here also the company developed a malt distillery, together with a large maturation, blending and bottling operation which now ensures the despatch to the four corners of the world of many millions of cases.

In all the company now owns eleven distilleries situated in different parts of Scotland and also its own malting in Kirkcaldy. Best known of its Scotch brands are Ballantine's, Old Smuggler and Grand Macnish, all of which have substantial sales in export markets and especially in Scandinavia. In Dumbarton, the company also operates an unusual security system. Taking a leaf out of history, it keeps a large flock of white geese, which stand guard over the hundreds of thousands of gallons in its warehouses, just as hundreds of years ago their forefathers protected the capitol in Rome.

There are many striking labels on Scotch whisky bottles. One of the more unusual shows the head and shoulders of an English monarch. This is King George IV, owned by The Distillers Agency Ltd, a subsidiary of DCL.

It is the individual carton used for this whisky, however, that carries the rare distinction of being 'approved' by the Vatican. The portrait of the King is reproduced from the painting by Thomas Lawrence which hangs in the Pinacoteca Vaticana in Rome, and special permission had to be obtained before it could be used.

Why King George IV for a Scotch whisky? Little seems to be known in the company of the reasons for the choice, but it is interesting that for many years the brand was bottled and blended at a plant at South Queensferry near Edinburgh where, in 1822, George IV came ashore as King of Scotland as well as of England on the first visit of an English monarch for over two hundred years.

Sir Walter Scott arranged the proceedings and gave the King a glass of whisky. Later he asked His Majesty for the glass so that he could take it home with him. Unfortunately, he forgot he had put the glass in a hip pocket, sat down suddenly, and broke it! In London the home of King George IV faces St. James's Palace, the birthplace of the monarch.

The famous names in the world of Scotch whisky

are not necessarily old ones. In fact, two of the best-known are comparative youngsters. These are Red Hackle and the Invergordon Distillers Group. As far as I can discover, they are the only whisky firms to have their own pipe bands. The Red Hackle Band is famous in the south of Scotland and is based on Glasgow; the Invergordon Pipe Band, from the Cromarty Firth, is in world championship class.

Red Hackle takes its name from the head-dress plume of small red feathers worn by the Black Watch regiment. The original partners in Hepburn and Ross, the founders of the Red Hackle firm, had served with the Black Watch and they chose their regiment's plume as their whisky's name. Their headquarters in Glasgow, Kelvin House, is a remarkable Scottish museum as well as a business centre.

The late Dr Charles Hepburn was a renowned collector of armour, antiques, tapestries and the like, and in the Red Hackle building you walk on a tartan carpet between knights in armour, stags' heads, shakos and helmets, broadswords, spears and cutlasses.

Invergordon Distillers are a very new firm indeed, since they came into the international market for Scotch whisky only some five or six years ago. Nevertheless they have some very old names with which to conjure. Their single malt, Deqnston Mill, is named after a mill built in 1785 about a mile up the River Teith from Castle Doune. The mill was later converted into a distillery. Their Islay malt, Bruichladdich, has been produced there for nearly a hundred years, and the distillery is the furthest west in Scotland – the next distillery west is in the United States of America!

Invergordon's Tullibardine Malt is made with water from the same source used to brew the ale for King James IV of Scotland after his coronation at Scone in 1488.

So fame in the world of Scotch whisky applies to new names as well as old ones, and praise comes for them from all over the globe.

The Red Hackle band in one of the company's distilleries.

Chapter 8

Scotch for the Hostess

Theodora FitzGibbon

Whisky has been the national drink of Scotland for many centuries. Indeed, on the Island of Lewis in the nineteenth century, tea-drinking was thought to be sinful and was only done in secret. The day started with a dram of whisky, known as a 'skalach' in the Highlands, and medical men denounced tea as dangerous to the nation's health, 'causing trembling and shaking of the head and hands, loss of appetite and other diseases'.

Food and drink go together, and in Scotland, as in many other European countries, the national drink is incorporated in the national *cuisine*. In many cases whisky is actually drunk with the food: at Hogmanay (New Year's Eve), when haggis is served to the swirl of a kilted Highlander playing the bagpipes, it is customary to drink small glasses of neat whisky between mouthfuls. The Scottish writer Tobias Smollett gives us a vivid description of a Highland breakfast in *The Expedition of Humphry Clinker* (1771), in which neither tea nor coffee appear.

> One kit of boiled eggs; a second, full of butter; a third, full of cream; an entire cheese made from goat's milk; a large earthen pot, full of honey; the best part of a ham; a cold venison pasty; a bushel of oatmeal, made into thin cakes and bannocks; with a small wheaten loaf in the middle, for the strangers; a stone bottle of whisky; another of brandy; and a kilderkin of ale.

Scotland's ties with France, the acknowledged home of great cooking, begin as far back as Charlemagne in the ninth century, and many Scottish dishes are French in origin, but adapted to Scottish tastes and ingredients. Whisky is, in fact, a much purer spirit than brandy and so can successfully be used in its place in many recipes.

The following is a selection of well tried national dishes and drinks, which will grace any table.

Opening the hampers at the shoot near Strathdon, Aberdeenshire, 1882.

99

Lunch at harvest-time, c. 1898.

Lobster à la Cleikum Club

Potted Trout

The Cleikum Club was a nineteenth-century Scottish club which specialised in good food. According to H. Jekyl, Esquire, a prominent member, this dish 'is one of those delicate messes which the gourmand loves to cook for himself in a silver dish held over a spirit-lamp, or in a silver stew-pan'.

*1 fresh lobster, cut in two   3 heaped tablespoons butter
   down the centre, lengthwise 4 tablespoons whisky,
½ pint cream   preferably pure malt
salt and pepper*

Remove the meat from the tail of the lobster and also from the claws and head. Then cut it into chunks. Heat the butter (preferably in a chafing dish), and when it is just foaming but not brown add the lobster, and seasoning.

Warm the whisky, and when the lobster is hot pour it over the lobster and set fire to it. Add the cream and mix with the pan juices, letting it heat gently but on no account boil, lest it should curdle. Put back in the half shells and serve hot. The shells can be put for a minute under a hot grill to brown slightly, but be careful not to allow them to dry up. *Serves 2.*

Crab and Dublin Bay prawns or scampi can be cooked in the same way.

Either brown or rainbow trout can be used. These fish will keep for some time in a cold place, if completely covered by the melted butter.

*12 trout   ¼ pint white wine vinegar
1 lb. butter   4 tablespoons whisky
a pinch each of mace, nutmeg salt and pepper
   and ground cloves*

Scale and clean the trout well. Wash them over with a little wine vinegar; slit them down the back and remove the backbone and other small rib bones. Sprinkle with salt and pepper, both inside and out, pour over the whisky and leave, covered, for several hours to absorb the marinade.

Put the trout head to tail in an ovenproof dish with a liberal nut of butter on each one, using about ½ lb. in all. Pour over the marinade of whisky and a few spoonfuls of the remaining wine vinegar, cover and bake them in a slow to moderate oven (275°F–300°F, gas mark 2–3) for 45 minutes. Take them out of the liquid carefully and put into a clean dish. When cold, cover them completely with the remainder of the butter which should first be melted with the mace, nutmeg and clove. Serve cold. *Serves 6.*

This recipe can also be used for herrings or mackerel.

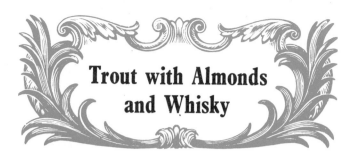

Trout with Almonds and Whisky

First clean and scale the fish, then roll them in the seasoned flour. Heat the butter and oil in a large frying pan and when they are just foaming, but not brown, put in the trout. Cook gently for about 5 minutes on each side. Then take out and put on to a warmed serving dish and keep warm. Add the almonds to the butter and toss lightly until hot and brown. Add the whisky, shaking the pan until the flame dies down. Add a squeeze of lemon juice, then pour over the trout and serve with the bananas split lengthways and lightly fried in butter. Add lemon wedges for garnish. *Serves 4.*

4 medium brown or rainbow trout
2 oz., flaked, toasted almonds
2 tablespoons butter
1 tablespoon oil
4 tablespoons whisky

seasoned flour
squeeze lemon juice
lemon wedges for garnish
4 bananas
2 tablespoons butter

Trout with Almonds and Whisky.

Tweed Kettle

Tweed Kettle or Salmon Hash is a nineteenth-century Edinburgh speciality.

3 lb. fresh salmon (tail-end is best)
2 chopped shallots or 2 tablespoons chopped chives
½ pint stock from the fish
salt and pepper
pinch of ground mace
2 tablespoons chopped parsley
4 tablespoons whisky
3 tablespoons cream (optional)

Put the fish into a kettle and cover with cold water. Add seasoning and a pinch of parsley. Bring to the boil and simmer for 5 minutes only. When cool, remove salmon, reserving the stock. Take all the skin and bones from the fish and cut it into cubes about 2 inches across. Season with a little more pepper, salt and the mace, then put into a saucepan with about 1 cup of the fish stock, the whisky and the shallots or chives. Cover and simmer very slowly for about 25 minutes. Add the cream and let it heat but not boil, then finally garnish with the parsley before serving either hot or cold. *Serves 4–6.*

Salmon steaks can be poached in water as above with the whisky added. Then either serve cold, or top with a knob of butter or the cream and put under a hot grill for 3 minutes. Garnish as above.

Fair Day at Benbecula, c. 1890.

Scotch Collops

Scotch Rarebit

4 veal chops or escallops of veal, well beaten
2 oz. finely sliced mushrooms
1 teaspoon tomato purée
2 teaspoons chopped parsley
1 small chopped shallot or onion
1 tablespoon each of butter and oil
2 tablespoons whisky
4 tablespoons chicken stock ($\frac{1}{2}$ cube will do)

Heat the butter and oil until foaming. Then brown the meat on both sides for about 3 minutes. Add the onion and let it soften, then put in the mushrooms and let them soften, without getting crisp. Add the whisky and flame it. Mix the purée into the stock, pour over the meat and season to taste. Cover and simmer gently for about 10 minutes, turning at least once. Garnish with parsley before serving. *Serves 4.*

Lamb or pork chops can also be used in this recipe.

This dish makes a delicious savoury.

$\frac{1}{2}$ lb. Dunlop or Cheddar cheese
$\frac{1}{2}$ oz. butter
2 teaspoons Worcestershire sauce
pepper
3 tablespoons whisky
1 level dessertspoon flour
$\frac{1}{2}$ teaspoon dry mustard

Grate the cheese and put into a thick-bottomed saucepan. Add the flour, mustard, Worcestershire sauce, butter and pepper. Mix well, then add the whisky to moisten, but do not make it too wet. Stir over a gentle heat until it is all melted. It should be quite a thickish paste – add a little more flour if it seems too thin. When shaken the mixture should leave the sides of the pan and swirl around. Toast 4 large rounds of toast on one side only, then spread the mixture on the untoasted side and brown under a hot grill. *Serves 4.*

Scotch Collops.

Roast Chicken Stuffed with Skirlie

Skirlie is a marvellous stuffing for poultry or lamb and very simple to make.

1 chicken, about 3–4 lb.	Skirlie
4 tablespoons whisky	*5 oz. coarse oatmeal*
1 cup giblet broth	*1 medium onion*
salt and pepper	*1 tablespoon chopped,*
sprig of tarragon	* fresh herbs such as*
4 tablespoons oil	* parsley, chives, thyme*
	2 oz. butter, margarine or
To flambé	* suet*
2 tablespoons warmed whisky	*½ teaspoon ground allspice*
	salt and pepper

First cover the giblets, except the liver, with salted water and boil gently for about ½ an hour. Strain, and reserve for future use. Put the chicken in a deep bowl with the chopped tarragon and pour over the whisky. Cover and leave for several hours, or overnight, turning at least once during that time.

Dry the oatmeal well in a low oven, then add the finely chopped onion, butter, herbs, allspice and seasoning. Add half the whisky marinade from the chicken and mix well. Stuff some into the crop end of the bird and the rest into the body. Secure with a small skewer. Put into a roasting tin, pour over the oil, and add some salt and pepper. Cover, either with foil or a lid, and roast in a moderate oven (350°F, gas mark 5–6) for about 1¼–1½ hours, removing the cover for the last half an hour to let the top brown. Put the bird on to a warmed serving dish and keep warm. Pour off any excess fat. Put the tin on top of the stove, add 1 cup of the giblet stock, the remainder of the whisky marinade, and seasoning to taste. Boil up rapidly until slightly reduced. At table, pour over the chicken a ladle of warmed whisky and let it flame. This dish is excellent without the final flambé, but for special occasions it makes a delectable meal. *Serves 4.*

Duck or **Goose** is also very good served as above. In the case of duck put 2 oranges, quartered (in their skin), around the bird after it has been cooking for ½ an hour.

In Scotland **Grouse** is not usually stuffed, but in the Highlands small wild raspberries, rowan-berries or cranberries are sometimes mixed with butter and about a tablespoon of whisky and put inside the bird. Sprigs of heather soaked in whisky are also placed outside the birds to give a special flavour. Sometimes rashers of bacon are wrapped around the heather during roasting.

Luncheon alfresco, c. 1860.

Chicken with Honey, Whisky and Almonds

1 roasting chicken, about	*2 oz. blanched sliced*
* 3–4 lb.*	* almonds*
3 tablespoons thick honey	*2 tablespoons oil*
3 tablespoons whisky,	*salt and pepper*
* preferably malt*	

First rub the whisky all over the bird, then dust it with salt and pepper. Line the roasting tin with a large piece of foil, enough to cover the bottom and sides and to come up right over the bird. Stand the chicken on the foil and add the leftover whisky. Rub the honey over the breast and legs, then sprinkle on the almonds. Finally pour the oil around the bird. Wrap it up and squeeze the top together so that it holds. Bake in a moderate oven (350°F, gas mark 6) for about 1¼–1½ hours, undoing the foil for 10 minutes at the end to brown the bird. Delicious hot or cold. *Serves 4–6.*

Tweed Kettle.

Chicken with Honey, Whisky and Almonds.

Chicken Pancakes with Whisky Sauce

Put the sifted flour and salt into a mixing bowl, then break the egg into the middle and mix well. Then gradually add the milk and beat with an egg beater until quite smooth. Finally add about 2 teaspoons cold water. Leave the pancake batter for about ½ an hour to get the air into it and beat it before use. Make the pancakes in the usual way; grease the pan. When it is hot add about 1 tablespoon of batter; once the batter is golden underneath, turn and brown the other side. Drain on paper and leave until needed for filling. (Makes 10 small pancakes.)

To make the filling, chop up the chicken and the mushrooms too, if they are large. Heat the butter and add the flour, letting it cook for 1 minute. Then gradually add the warmed milk, stirring all the time until it is smooth and creamy. Turn the heat very low, then add the chicken and mushrooms. Season to taste and simmer gently until the mushrooms are soft. Add the whisky and the chopped parsley. Leave to get cold.

Now divide this mixture between the pancakes, roll them up and put side by side in an ovenproof dish. Heat the butter and when just oily add the tablespoon of whisky. Pour this over the top of the pancakes and put into a hot oven (400°F, gas mark 8) for about 15 minutes or until hot through. *Serves 4–5.*

This is an excellent way of using up leftovers.

Pancakes

5 oz. flour	*pinch of salt*
1 egg	*a few drops of water*
¼ pint milk	*a little butter for frying*

Filling

2 cups cooked chicken (or	*3 tablespoons whisky*
a mixture of chicken	*2 teaspoons chopped*
and ham)	*parsley*
¼ lb. mushrooms	*salt and pepper*
2 tablespoons butter	*2 tablespoons melted butter*
2 tablespoons flour	*mixed with 1 tablespoon*
1 pint warm milk	*whisky*

Chicken Pancakes with Whisky Sauce.

Kidneys Flambé

Heat the butter until it is foaming. Then add the prepared kidneys, cut in half, or in four if they are veal
kidneys. Let them brown well on all sides, turning them
frequently. Mix together the whisky, lemon juice,
mustard, salt and pepper and pour over the kidneys in
the hot pan. If it does not flame, set alight. Turn the
kidneys well in the sauce, and scrape down the sides of
the pan. Sprinkle with parsley before serving. *Serves
2–3.*

6 lamb's kidneys, or 3 veal
   kidneys
2 oz. butter
½ teaspoon made mustard
salt and black pepper

juice of ½ lemon
2–3 tablespoons whisky
a little chopped parsley
   for garnish

Kidneys Flambé.

Christmas Whisky Cake

6 oz. candied peel
6 oz. glacé cherries
4 oz. almonds
1 lb. sultanas
1 lb. currants
12 oz. raisins
10 oz. plain flour
10 oz. butter

10 oz. soft brown sugar
1 tablespoon black treacle
grated rind of 1 lemon and
   1 orange
½ teaspoon each of grated
   nutmeg and mixed spice
6 tablespoons whisky
6 eggs

Blanch and chop the almonds; chop the peel and the cherries. Coat all the dried fruit with a little flour in a large bowl and add the nuts. Cream the butter and sugar until light in a separate bowl, then add the grated lemon and orange rind and finally the treacle. Beat the eggs well and add them gradually, with a scattering of flour on each; beat them again with a wooden spoon. Add the rest of the flour sifted with the spices and the alcohol to a consistency that will drop when shaken from the spoon. Lastly stir in the fruit and mix well.

   Grease and line a 9-inch cake tin and put the mixture into it, making a slight depression in the centre to prevent it rising too much. Cover with 2 thicknesses of greaseproof paper to slow the browning process. Bake at 325°F, gas mark 3 for 20 minutes, then reduce to 300°F, gas mark 2 for 40 minutes, then to 275°F, gas mark 1 for the remainder of the cooking time, about another 4 hours. Let the cake cool for an hour before taking it from the tin and cooling on a wire rack. Leave for at least 1 week before putting on the marzipan and a further week before icing.

Peaches in Whisky Syrup

16 fresh peaches
1 lb. caster sugar
2 pints water

6 tablespoons whisky,
   preferably malt

Put the peaches into a large bowl and pour enough water over to cover. Leave for about 5 minutes, lift out gently and peel off the skin. Put the sugar into the water, bring to the boil and simmer gently for about 15 minutes, or until slightly reduced. Add the peaches and poach them gently for about 15 minutes, turning them carefully with a slotted spoon. Transfer to the bowl from which they will be served, add the whisky to the syrup and boil hard for 5 minutes. Cool slightly then pour over the peaches and chill before serving. *Serves 8.*

Christmas Whisky Cake.

Peaches in Whisky Syrup.

Atholl Brose

Atholl Brose Syllabub

Atholl Brose is named after the Duke of Atholl who captured in 1475 his great enemy, the Earl of Ross, by filling the well at which Ross was known to drink with this potent libation. Ross drank deeply of this magical liquor and was taken while sleeping off the effects. This recipe was given by the Eighth Duke of Atholl. Although this is a drink, a pleasant dessert can be made from it (see the next recipe).

3 heaped tablespoons oatmeal	approx. 1 pint water
2 tablespoons liquid heather honey	whisky to make up 1 quart

Put the oatmeal into a bowl and mix with the water until it is a thick paste. Let it stand for about $\frac{1}{2}$–1 hour. Then put it through a fine strainer, pressing down well with a spoon so that the oatmeal is quite dry. Throw away the meal and mix the liquid with the runny honey. Stir with a *silver* spoon until well blended and the honey is absorbed. Pour into a quart bottle and fill up with whisky. Cork well, and always shake before using.

Atholl Brose and Syllabub.

Pour 4 tablespoons of the above into 4 tall glasses (1 to each glass) and fill up with whipped sweetened cream. Sprinkle the top with lightly toasted oatmeal and a dust of nutmeg. Chill and serve with small macaroons. *Serves 4.*

Caledonian Cream

A nineteenth-century Highland sweet.

1 lb. soft curds or cottage cheese	2 tablespoons sugar
2 heaped tablespoons Dundee marmalade	2 tablespoons malt whisky
	1 tablespoon lemon juice

Mix all the ingredients together, very thoroughly, and beat with a whisk. Put into a dish and freeze. *Serves 4–6.*

Cranachan

2 heaped tablespoons toasted oatmeal	2 tablespoons sugar
$\frac{1}{2}$ lb. cottage cheese or $\frac{1}{4}$ pint cream or equivalent ice-cream	2–3 tablespoons malt whisky

Sieve the cottage cheese and beat well. If using cream, then whip until frothy but not stiff. Toast the oatmeal lightly under a slow grill until crisp but not brown, and mix all the ingredients together. Freeze until firm. *Serves 4.*

Scottish Black Bun

Black Bun is a rich and delicious fruit cake formerly eaten on Twelfth Night, but nowadays served at Hogmanay (New Year's Eve). Like a Christmas Cake, it should be made several weeks before it is wanted, so that it can mature.

Mix all the filling ingredients together except the milk. Then add just enough milk to moisten the mixture. Make the pastry in the usual way and put on to a floured board, rolling it out to a thin sheet. Grease a tin 8–9 inches square (or 2 smaller ones) and cut the pastry into two pieces, one twice the size of the other.

Line the tin with the larger half. Put in the filling and the pastry lid on top, damping the edges well to make it stick. Prick all over with a fork, brush with the beaten egg and cook in a slow oven (275°F–290°F, gas mark 2) for about 3–4 hours. Leave in the tin until cold before removing. Black Bun will keep well in an airtight tin.

Casing

1 lb. self-raising flour
8 oz. butter

1 beaten egg for finishing
a little cold water

Filling

2 lb. seedless raisins
3 lb. currants
½ lb. chopped blanched almonds
3/4 lb. flour
½ lb. sugar
2 teaspoons Jamaica pepper (allspice)
1 teaspoon ground ginger

1 teaspoon ground cinnamon
¼ teaspoon black pepper
1 flat teaspoon cream of tartar
1 flat teaspoon baking powder
2 tablespoons whisky
approx. ¼ pint milk

Raw materials for Scottish Black Bun.

Toddy

'Sit roun' the table well content
An' steer aboot the toddy.'

This is a traditional recipe, and can be recommended for a bad head cold.

3–4 lumps sugar   *boiling whisky*
boiling water   *slice of lemon*

First warm a tumbler, then put in 3 or 4 lumps of sugar (or equivalent granulated) and pour over a wine-glass of boiling water. When dissolved add the same amount of whisky and stir with a silver spoon. Add more boiling water and a second glass of whisky. Stir again and sip the toddy 'with slow and loving care'!

Nowadays a slice of lemon is added and a spoonful of honey is sometimes used instead of the sugar.

In the old days whisky was also added to milkless, sweetened tea, and a sprinkle of nutmeg put on top. This is known as Birse Tea. It was also drunk in a glass of fresh cream sweetened with heather honey and called *Mairi Bhan*.

Whisky Punch

Another old favourite and it can be served hot or cold.

Hot punch:
Make tea by infusing 6 tablespoons in 1 quart of boiling water, then strain it over 1 lb lump sugar and a very thinly sliced lemon in a large bowl. Stir with a silver spoon and add 1 bottle of whisky. Set alight and serve in punch glasses.

Cold punch:
Peel 3 lemons finely and squeeze out the juice, then put them in a large jug with ½ lb. sugar. Pour 2 pints boiling water over and leave until cold. Strain into a large punch bowl and add a bottle of whisky, stirring very well. Chill for at least 1 hour before serving.

Het Pint

Het Pint is one of the old traditional, delicious Hogmanay drinks. It used to be carried through the streets in large copper kettles, known as toddy kettles, several hours before midnight. Sir Walter Scott wrote that 'it was uncanny and would certainly have felt very uncomfortable, not to welcome the New Year in the midst of the family, and a few old friends, with the immemorial libation of a het pint.'

4 pints mild ale   *3 eggs*
1 teaspoon grated nutmeg   *½ pint whisky*
4 oz. caster sugar

Put the ale into a thick saucepan. Then add the nutmeg and bring to just below boiling-point. Stir in the sugar and let it dissolve. Beat the eggs very well and add them gradually to the beer, stirring all the time so that it doesn't curdle. Then add the whisky and heat it up, but on no account let it boil, or the alcohol content will be lowered. Pour the liquid back and forth from the saucepan into warmed tankards, so that it becomes clear and sparkling.

Whisky Punch.

Auld Man's Milk

Whisky Butter

This is Meg Dod's recipe for Auld Man's Milk – the origin of the American eggnog. Meg Dods was the pseudonym of Christian Isobel Johnstone who was born in Fife in 1781 and died in 1857. She wrote *The Cook and Housewife's Manual* in 1826, which subsequently went into many editions. Mrs Johnstone was a great friend of Sir Walter Scott and other Scottish notables.

6 eggs, separated   1 pint whisky
4 pints of milk or thin cream   a pinch of nutmeg

Beat the egg yolks with the milk and stir in the whisky. Then fold in the whipped whites and put into a punch-bowl. Sprinkle with nutmeg before serving.

Everyone has a favourite recipe for Christmas Pudding, and it will be even more delicious if you use whisky as the spirit and also to flame it. Whisky Butter is traditionally served with Christmas Pudding and mince-pies in Scotland.

½ lb. unsalted butter   a small pinch of nutmeg
6 oz. caster sugar   6 tablespoons whisky,
squeeze of lemon juice   preferably malt

Cream the butter until it is light in colour, then beat the sugar in gradually. When well mixed, add the lemon juice and the whisky gradually a few drops at a time, beating continuously. Finally add the nutmeg and pile up in a dish. Chill before serving.

Golfers at the nineteenth hole, c. 1890.

Highland Cordial

This a traditional drink popular with the Victorians. It needs three months to reach maturity, but will in fact keep much longer.

1 lb. white currants *2 pints whisky*
rind of 2 lemons *1 lb. lump sugar*
a walnut-sized piece of root
*   ginger well bruised*

Strip the currants off the stalks and put into a large jug or container with the thin lemon rind and bruised ginger. Then add the whisky and mix well. Cover and let it stand for 48 hours, then strain and add the sugar, stirring well. Leave to stand until the sugar is dissolved, then bottle and cork well. Leave for 3 months to get the best results.

Hogmanannie

A drink for New Year's morning. The name Hogmanay is thought to have come from the Old French *aguil' anneuf* through Norman-French *hoguigané* to 'the New Year'.

2 eggs, separated *2 tablespoons cream*
2 tablespoons caster sugar *4 double Scotch whiskies*

Separate the whites and yolks of 2 eggs and beat up the yolks with 2 tablespoons of caster sugar and 2 tablespoons of cream. Whip the whites until fairly stiff. Add 4 double Scotch whiskies to the yolks and finally stir in the whites before serving.

Highland Special

3 measures of whisky, 2 measures of dry French vermouth, 2 tablespoons orange juice, all well mixed and served with a little grated nutmeg.

Highland Cooler

A good long drink which consists of: 1 teaspoon caster sugar, the juice of ½ lemon, 2 dashes of Angostura bitters, 1 measure of whisky and a cube of ice. Full up with ginger ale.

Whisky Mac

Wonderful on a cold day.

Whisky Mac is made from whisky and Crabbie's green ginger wine in the ratio of equal proportions or two-thirds whisky to one-third ginger wine if preferred.

Whisky Tom Collins

Juice of ½ lemon, 1 double whisky, 1 egg white, 2–3 large lumps of ice. Shake well, pour into a tall glass and fill up with soda water.

Scotch Rickey

1 lump of ice, the juice of $\frac{1}{2}$ a lime and a quarter of a lemon to one double whisky. Shake well, pour into a tall glass and fill up with soda water.

Rob Roy

Equal parts of Italian vermouth and whisky with 2 drops of Angostura bitters served over ice cubes.

Whisky Sour

1 double measure of whisky, the juice of $\frac{1}{2}$ lemon and a pinch of sugar. Add the white of an egg, shake with ice and serve with a dash of soda water. This can be made without the egg white, but is better with it.

Purple Heather

An invention of my own which I think is delicious. To one measure of whisky add the juice of $\frac{1}{2}$ lemon and 3 teaspoons of blackcurrant syrup or Cassis. Pour into a tall glass and fill up with soda water.

Self-portrait of D. Octavius Hill with friends, Edinburgh, 1845.

THE DISTILLERIES OF SCOTLAND

See page 41 for a map of the distilleries

LOWLAND MALT

1	Auchentoshan	*Eadie Cairns Ltd*
2	Bladnoch	*Bladnoch Distillery Ltd*
3	Glenkinchie	*John Haig & Co. Ltd*
4	Inverleven	*Hiram Walker & Sons (Scotland) Ltd*
5	Kinclaith	*Long John Distilleries Ltd*
6	Ladyburn	*Wm Grant & Sons Ltd*
7	Littlemill	*Barton Distilling (Scotland) Ltd*
8	Lomond	*Hiram Walker & Sons (Scotland) Ltd*
9	Rosebank	*The Distillers Agency Ltd*
10	St Magdalene	*John Hopkins & Co. Ltd*
11	Moffat	*Inver House Distillers Ltd*

ISLAY MALT

12	Ardbeg	*Ardbeg Distillery Ltd*
13	Bowmore	*Sherriff's Bowmore Distillery Ltd*
14	Bruichladdich	*Bruichladdich Distillery Co. Ltd*
15	Bunnahabhain	*The Highland Distilleries Co. Ltd*
16	Caol Ila	*Bulloch Lade & Co. Ltd*
17	Lagavulin	*White Horse Distilleries Ltd*
18	Laphroaig	*D. Johnston & Co. (Laphroaig) Ltd*
19	Port Ellen	*Low Robertson & Co. Ltd*

GRAIN

20	Ben Nevis	*Ben Nevis Distillery (Fort William) Ltd*
21	Caledonian	*Scottish Grain Distillers Ltd*
22	Cambus	*Scottish Grain Distillers Ltd*
23	Cameronbridge	*Scottish Grain Distillers Ltd*
24	Carsebridge	*Scottish Grain Distillers Ltd*
25	Dumbarton	*Hiram Walker & Sons (Scotland) Ltd*
26	Girvan	*Wm Grant & Sons Ltd*
27	Invergordon	*The Invergordon Distillers Ltd*
28	Lochside	*Macnab Distilleries Ltd*
29	Moffat	*Inver House Distillers Ltd*
30	North British	*North British Distillery Co. Ltd*
31	Port Dundas	*Scottish Grain Distillers Ltd*
32	Strathclyde	*Long John Distilleries Ltd*
33	North of Scotland	*North of Scotland Distilling Co. Ltd*

CAMPBELTOWN MALT

34	Glen Scotia	*A. Gillies & Co. (Distillers) Ltd*
35	Springbank	*J. & A. Mitchell & Co. Ltd*

HIGHLAND MALT

36	Aberfeldy	*John Dewar & Sons Ltd*
37	Aberlour-Glenlivet	*Aberlour-Glenlivet Distillery Co. Ltd*
38	Ardmore	*Wm Teacher & Sons Ltd*
39	Aultmore	*John & Robt Harvey & Co. Ltd*
40	Balblair	*Balblair Distillery Co. Ltd*
41	Balmenach	*John Crabbie & Co. Ltd*
42	Balvenie	*Wm Grant & Sons Ltd*
43	Banff	*Slater, Rodger & Co. Ltd*
44	Ben Nevis	*Ben Nevis Distillery (Fort William) Ltd*
45	Ben Riach-Glenlivet	*The Longmorn-Glenlivet Distilleries Ltd*
46	Benrinnes	*A. & A. Crawford Ltd*
47	Benromach	*J. & W. Hardie Ltd*

48	Ben Wyvis	*The Invergordon Distillers Ltd*
49	Blair Athol	*Arthur Bell & Sons Ltd*
50	Caperdonich	*The Glenlivet & Glen Grant Distillers Ltd*
51	Cardow	*John Walker & Sons Ltd*
52	Clynelish	*Ainslie & Heilbron (Distillers) Ltd*
53	Coleburn	*J. & G. Stewart Ltd*
54	Convalmore	*W. P. Lowrie & Co. Ltd*
55	Cragganmore	*D. & J. McCallum Ltd*
56	Craigellachie	*White Horse Distillers Ltd*
57	Dailuaine	*Dailuaine-Talisker Distilleries Ltd*
58	Dallas Dhu	*Benmore Distilleries Ltd*
59	Dalmore	*Mackenzie Bros., Dalmore, Ltd*
60	Dalwhinnie	*James Buchanan & Co. Ltd*
61	Deanston	*Deanston Distillers Ltd*
62	Dufftown-Glenlivet	*Arthur Bell & Sons Ltd*
63	Edradour	*Wm Whiteley Ltd*
64	Fettercairn	*Fettercairn Distillery Ltd*
65	Glen Albyn	*Mackinlays & Birnie Ltd*
66	Glenallachie	*Mackinlay-McPherson Ltd*
67	Glenburgie-Glenlivet	*James & George Stodart Ltd*
68	Glencadam	*George Ballantine & Son Ltd*
69	Glendronach	*Glendronach Distillery Co. Ltd*
70	Glendullan	*Macdonald Greenlees Ltd*
71	Glen Elgin	*White Horse Distillers Ltd*
72	Glenfarclas-Glenlivet	*J. & G. Grant Ltd*
73	Glenfiddich	*Wm Grant & Sons Ltd*
74	Glenglassaugh	*The Highland Distilleries Co. Ltd*
75	Glengoyne	*Lang Brothers Ltd*
76	Glen Grant-Glenlivet	*J. & J. Grant, Glen Grant Ltd*
77	Glen Keith-Glenlivet	*Chivas Bros. Ltd*
78	Glenlivet, The	*George & J. G. Smith Ltd*
79	Glenlossie	*John Haig & Co. Ltd*
80	Glen Mhor	*Mackinlays & Birnie Ltd*
81	Glenmorangie	*Macdonald & Muir Ltd*
82	Glen Moray-Glenlivet	*Macdonald & Muir Ltd*
83	Glenrothes-Glenlivet	*The Highland Distilleries Co. Ltd*
84	Glen Spey	*W. & A. Gilbey Ltd*
85	Glentauchers	*James Buchanan & Co. Ltd*
86	Glenturret	*Glenturret Distillery Ltd*
87	Glenugie	*Long John Distilleries Ltd*
88	Glenury-Royal	*John Gillon & Co. Ltd*
89	Highland Park	*James Grant & Co. (Highland Park Distillery) Ltd*
90	Hillside	*Wm Sanderson & Son Ltd*
91	Imperial	*Dailuaine-Talisker Distilleries Ltd*
92	Inchgower	*Arthur Bell & Sons Ltd*
93	Isle of Jura	*Isle of Jura Distillery Co. Ltd*
94	Knockando	*Justerini & Brooks Ltd*
95	Knockdhu	*James Munro & Son Ltd*
96	Linkwood	*John McEwan & Co. Ltd*
97	Loch Lomond	*Barton Distilling (Scotland) Ltd*
98	Lochside	*Macnab Distilleries Ltd*
99	Longmorn-Glenlivet	*The Longmorn-Glenlivet Distilleries Ltd*
100	Macallan-Glenlivet	*R. Kemp, Macallan-Glenlivet Ltd*
101	Macduff	*Glendeveron Distillers Ltd*
102	Millburn	*Macleay Duff (Distillers) Ltd*
103	Miltonduff-Glenlivet	*George Ballantine & Son Ltd*
104	Mortlach	*George Cowie & Son Ltd*
105	North Port	*Mitchell Brothers Ltd*
106	Ord	*Peter Dawson Ltd*
107	Pulteney	*James & George Stodart Ltd*
108	Royal Brackla	*John Bisset & Co. Ltd*
109	Royal Lochnagar	*John Begg Ltd*
110	Scapa	*Taylor & Ferguson Ltd*
111	Speyburn	*John Robertson & Son Ltd*
112	Strathisla-Glenlivet	*Chivas Brothers Ltd*
113	Strathmill	*Justerini & Brooks Ltd*
114	Talisker	*Dailuaine-Talisker Distilleries Ltd*

115	Tamdhu-Glenlivet	*The Highland Distilleries Co. Ltd*	
116	Tamnavulin-Glenlivet	*Tamnavulin-Glenlivet Distillery Co. Ltd*	
117	Teaninich	*R. H. Thomson & Co. (Distillers) Ltd*	
118	Tomatin	*Tomatin Distillers Co. Ltd*	
119	Tomintoul-Glenlivet	*The Tomintoul-Glenlivet Distillery Ltd*	
120	Tormore	*Long John Distilleries Ltd*	
121	Tullibardine	*Tullibardine Distillery Ltd*	
122	Auchroisk	*International Distillers & Vintners Ltd*	
123	Ledaig	*Ledaig Distillery (Tobermory) Ltd*	
124	Glenlochy	*Scottish Malt Distillers Ltd*	
125	Mannochmore	*John Haig & Co. Ltd*	
126	Oban	*William Greer & Co. Ltd*	
127	Glen Garioch	*The Glen Garioch Distillery Co. Ltd*	
128	Speyside	*Speyside Distillery Co. Ltd*	
129	Glen Foyle	*Brodie Hepburn Ltd*	

Acknowledgments

Arthur Bell & Son (Perth) Ltd 93(bottom); British Tourist Authority 35(top), 37, 38(top right), 39(top left & right, bottom); Bryan & Shear 33, 94; James Buchanan & Sons Ltd 19, 62(bottom); Eadie Cairns Ltd 40(bottom right); Camera Press (John Drysdale) 45(top left); Cathcart Collection, National Museum of Antiquities of Scotland 113; Country Life Archive, National Museum, Edinburgh 87; Distillers Company Ltd 12–13, 34(bottom), 38(top left), 44(top right), 45(top right), 47(left & right), 49–50(bottom), 52, 53(top), 57(top & bottom), 60(bottom left), 63(bottom), 66(bottom), 69(centre), 77(top right), 79, 91(top left & right, bottom); Mary Evans Picture Library 15, 24–5, 29, 30(bottom), 72, 74(top), 85, 96(bottom); Matthew Gloag & Sons Ltd 74, 78, 79; William Grant & Co. Ltd 40(top), 44(bottom left & right), 48(top & bottom right), 56(top left), 57(top & bottom), 60(top), 76(top left), 80(top right); Susan Griggs 36(top); John Hannavy 36(bottom); John Hillelson 56(top right); IDV 45(bottom left), 64, 84(bottom); Keystone Press Agency (Chris Ware) 59; Mansell Collection 26, 30(bottom right), 86(right); George Morrison 98–115 inclusive; National Museum of Antiquities of Scotland 16, 17(top & bottom left); National Trust for Scotland 20; Picturepoint 44(top left); Radio Times Hulton Picture Library 14, 21, 23, 27, 28, 50(top), 51, 63(top), 90; Robertson & Baxter Ltd 67(bottom); Barry Salter 33, 54–5; Wm Sanderson Ltd 18, 84; Scotch Whisky Association 7, 9, 40, 43, 68(top), 69(top); Scottish Tourist Authority 35(bottom); J & G Stewart Ltd 83; Wm Teacher & Sons Ltd 81(bottom), 93(top); Tomatin Distillers Ltd 70(top & bottom); Victoria & Albert Museum 42; Johnnie Walker & Sons Ltd 22, 31(top & bottom), 45(bottom), 46(bottom), 48, 57, 62(top left), 68(bottom), 85, 88, 89.

Index